Everyday Life in

Tudor Shrewsbury

By Bill Champion

Shropshire Books

Front Cover
The Market Hall, 1596, and Lloyd's Mansion, 1570
(from a painting by Thomas Shotter Boys, 1859).
In Tudor times the houses in the High Street would
have been obscured by the Guildhall.

Back cover
The Burghley map, c. 1575
(from a lithograph in the Local Studies Library, Shrewsbury)

ISBN: 0-903802-60-0
© Bill Champion 1994
Cover and book design: Paul Brasenell
Managing Editor: Helen Sample
Published by Shropshire Books, the Publishing Division of the
Leisure Services Department of Shropshire County Council.
Printed by Livesey Limited

About the author

Bill Champion's connections with Shrewsbury came about by accident. Born less than fifty miles north of the equator in Uganda, he first came to Shrewsbury as a boarder at the Schools on Kingsland, going on to university to read History.
Hopes of writing a thesis on Tudor Shrewsbury had to be put aside, but a recent opportunity to contribute as a freelance to the forthcoming volume on the county town for the Victoria County History of Shropshire rekindled his interest. This book is a by-product of the research for that project. At present the author lives in the Erging district of Herefordshire, far enough away to take a detached, but hopefully sympathetic view of the otherwise forgotten lives of Tudor 'proud Salopians'.

Acknowledgements

For assistance in writing this book I would like to acknowledge the help of Marion Roberts, Ruth Bagley and their staff at the Shropshire Record Office, past and present, as well as that given by the staff at the Guildhall in Dogpole who brought up records for my examination. My debt to Tony Carr and his colleagues at the Local Studies Library in Castle Gates is equally great: the selection of photos and drawings in particular was made much easier with their advice. The illustrations of the covered way from the Sextry and of Jones's Mansion are reproduced by courtesy of the British Library; that of Colle Hall by courtesy of the Bodleian Library. The reproduction on the cover of Lloyd's Mansion and the Market Hall is taken from the painting by Shotter Boys with permission of Shrewsbury Museum.

Several illustrations have also been redrawn for this book by Kathryn Green from reproductions of old prints and other sources. All other illustrations are reproduced with kind permission from Shropshire Records & Research Department. For invaluable information and for reading and commenting on part or whole of the text, I would also like to thank James Lawson, Alan Somerset, George Baugh, Madge Moran, Eric Mercer and Penny Berryman. Readers who would like to investigate Tudor Shrewsbury further should certainly consult the Shropshire volumes, edited by Professor Somerset, in the series *Records of Early English Drama*, which are in the press as I write. These contain full transcripts of the documents relating to several of the incidents mentioned in this book, such as the Shearmen's tree.

Contents

	Page
Map of Tudor Shrewsbury	*viii-ix*
Preface	*xi*

Chapter 1 - Time and Calendar — 1
Bringing in the tree — 1
Curfew and the watch — 3
The daily rhythm — 5
The Salopian calendar — 6

Chapter 2 - Authority — 13
Petitions and submission — 13
'Michaelmas gents' — 15
Council and Commons — 16
Privilege of the people — 20

Chapter 3 - Population, Trade and Markets — 23
A growing population — 23
The impact of plague — 25
The great rebuilding — 27
Markets and fairs — 32

Chapter 4 - Households and Companies — 37
Households — 37
Schooling — 38
Service — 41
Setting up shop — 43
Courtship and marriage — 45
Companies and guilds — 48

Chapter 5 - Presentments and Neighbours — 51
The Great Court — 51
Streeters' bills — 52
Affrays and bloods — 54
Peace bonds — 56
Drains and rights of way — 58

Chapter 6 - Going to Law — 59
The Small Court — 59
Process and tickets — 60
Saving harmless — 61
Prison — 62
Prynce of Abbey Foregate — 65
Juries and wager of law — 67

Chapter 7 - Making a Living — 69
Trades, streets and housing — 69
Wool and cloth — 72
Friezing, cottoning and shearing — 75
Cappers and fullers — 76
Victuals and dearth — 77
'First-brewed Shrewsbury ale' — 79
Carpentry and brick — 82
Trows and float waters — 84
Gambling Dick — 86

Chapter 8 - Crime and the Common Peace — 89
Felonies and misdemeanours — 89
Assizes and sessions — 92
Trial and the gallows — 93
The Council in the Marches — 95

Chapter 9 - Church and Reformation — 99
Purgatory, priests and the saints — 99
By faith alone — 103
A city on the hill? — 106
From Corpus Christi to Shrewsbury Show — 109

Epilogue — 111
Memory and place — 111

Map of Tudor Shrewsbury

Town wall with towers
(some positions conjectural)

Bridges

M St. Mary's church
A St. Alkmund's church
J St. Julian's church
C St. Chad's church
G Guildhall and Exchequer
FD Dominican Friary (Black Friars)
FF Franciscan Friary (Grey Friars)
FA Augustinian Friary (Austin Friars)
CG Castle Gates (upper and lower)
WG Welsh Gate
SG Stone Gate
+ High Cross
m mills (Stone Bridge and Abbey mills)

Postern Gates listed in 1451

P1 At Cripplelode
P2 Next to the Austin Friars
P3 At Claremont
P4 Called 'Shoplatch gate'
P5 Opposite Kayme's place
(in Murivance)
P6 Next to Stury's close
P7 At Bulgerlode
P8 At St. Mary's Waterlode

Other postern gates are also known:

P9 At the end of Beeches Lane
P10 Beside the main gate
to the Grey Friars (both vaulted)
P11 Opposite St. Mary's Church
P12 Leading to Roushill meadows
Beside the Castle Gate
(not shown on map)

1. Shearmen's Hall
and Proude's Mansion
2. Gullet tavern
3. Sextry tavern
4. Thornes' Place
5. Sherer's Mansion
6. Worrall's House
7. Ireland's Mansion
8. Owen's Mansion
9. Jones's Mansion (Dogpole)
10. Perche's Mansion
11. Rowley's House and Mansion
12. Drapers' Hall
13. Grammar School and Rigg's Hall
14. Lloyd's Mansion
15. Gibbons's Mansion
16. Jones's Mansion (Under the Wyle)
17. Merivale House
18. Bellstone Hall
19. The Stone House
20. Bennett's Hall
21. Market Hall (1596)
22. St. John's Hospital (Cole almshouses)
23. Colle (Cole) Hall
24. The Red Lion
25. Romaldesham Hall
26. 'Henry Tudor' House
27. The Abbot's House
28. 127 Frankwell
29. Fellmongers' Hall
30. Old Liberal Club
31. Council House
32. St. Mary's almshouses
33. St. Chad's almshouses
34. Round Tower near the Austin Friars
35. Garewald's Tower
36. Mardol Quay

Wards and Main Streets (based on Great Court listings)

Stone Ward

Abbey Foregate
(incorporated in the Stone Ward in 1586)
Coleham
Stone Bridge
Under the Wyle
The Wyle
Wyle Cop (including Milk Street -
mentioned in 1629)
Dogpole (part)

High Street (south side) with Baxters Row
Cornmarket (now The Square)
Kiln Lane (now Princess Street)
Murivance (now Swan Hill)

Welsh Ward

Frankwell
Mardol
Knockyn Street (now Hill's Lane)
Romaldesham (now Barker Street -
mentioned in 1530 - and Bridge Street)
Claremont (now Claremont Hill)
Doglane (now Claremont Street)
St. John's Hill
Shoplatch
Lastalles (from Mardol Head to the junction
with Roushill)

Castle Ward

Castle Foregate
High Pavement (now Castle Street)
with The Bayly and Rotten Lane
(now School Gardens)
St. Mary's Churchyard and Dogpole (part)*
Corvisors Row (now Pride Hill -
mentioned in 1445)**
Fish Street (including Butcher Row -
mentioned in 1383)
High Street (north side)*

* Until the seventeenth century,
Great Court listings included the
Castle Ward portions of Dogpole
and High Street within the
Stone Ward.

** In the Middle Ages, Corvisors Row
had described what is now the north
side of Pride Hill; but in Tudor times
it clearly described, at least for
administrative purposes, both sides
of the street as far as the High Cross.

Other lanes marked on map:

gl Grope Lane
cl Carnarvon Lane
rl Roushill Lane

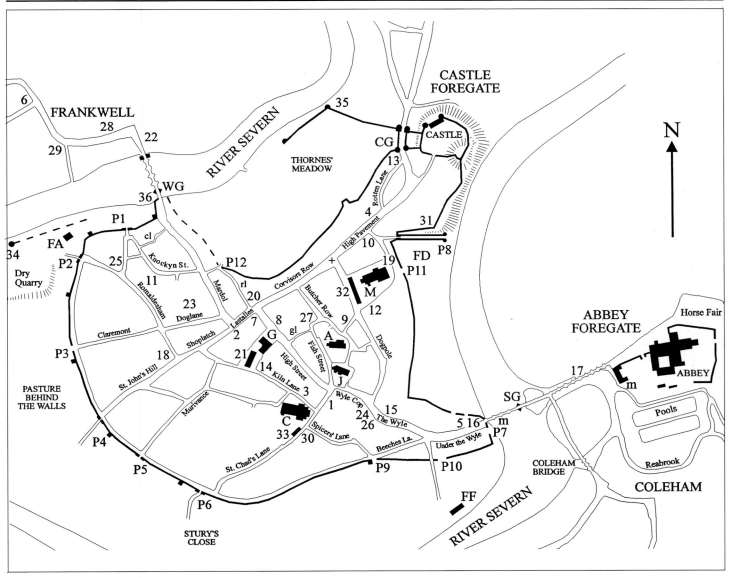

Map of Tudor Shrewsbury

Preface

Shrewsbury's past is among the best documented of any town in the country, and this is especially true for the Tudor period. In a book of this size it is impossible to do justice to all the incidents which these records describe, or to the many interesting characters they bring to light. Of the examples omitted, the case of the protestant refugees Madern and Gyllam Wisbecke is just one that comes to mind. They emigrated to England from France around the mid sixteenth century and settled in Shrewsbury - one becoming a joiner and popular physician, the other also a noted joiner whose wainscot work can still be seen at the Drapers' Hall. Then there was the London merchant William Langley who during business trips to his native county in 1606 avidly courted the nubile Hester Barkley of Shrewsbury, much to the disgust of some of the local apprentices who had a crush on her: *'Cannot William Langley get him a wife in London but must fetch our weather from hence?'* as one complained. Seeing that Langley was both bald and had a withered leg, a witty but cruel lampoon in prose verse was composed at his expense by *'Rodento Lento'*, alias the apprentice Peter Studley, begging Hester to *'Affect therefore some one of better nature, let love and reason rule thy heart therein, let not thy father choose a crooked creature for to embrace thy alabaster skin'*. The libellous paper was then stuck into a broom behind the door of a draper's shop and, after its discovery, was passed around the town, to the malicious guffaws of more than one Salopian.

Details such as these help bring to life the experience of Shrewsbury townsfolk some four hundred years ago, and I hope that others described in this book will do the same. At the same time I am conscious that more could have been said about material conditions; to compare, for instance, the sparse furnishings of the poor - perhaps a bed, table and form (no chairs), and some basic linen - with the cushions, Arras tapestries, silver spoons and showy plate of the rich as itemized in their probate inventories. But some selection has been necessary, and in this respect I have tried to concentrate upon aspects of daily life such as going to law and the regulation of communal life which, although unfamiliar to us today, were all-important to Salopians of the time.

Finally, a few general points: although this book is about Tudor Shrewsbury (i.e. 1485-1603), in practice I have used evidence from before or after those dates if the continuity of the subject needed it. In Tudor times, as today, Salopians talked of St. Julian's church, a usage which I have employed too although in fact the original and proper dedication was to St. Juliana's. Full references to the sources used in this book may be obtained from a typescript of the text to be deposited in Shrewsbury Local Studies Library. Anyone who cannot remember the introduction of decimalisation in 1972 might find it helpful to note some of the main conversion values between the old and new money.

> 1d = 1/2 new pence;
> 6d = 2 1/2 new pence;
> 12d (one shilling, 1s) = 5 new pence;
> 2s = 10 new pence;
> 10s = 50 new pence;
> 20s (£1) = 100 new pence (£1).

Chapter 1 - Time and Calendar

Bringing in the tree

'This year [1589] *in the month of May and June was some controversy in the town of Salop about the setting up of maypoles and bonfires making and erection of trees before the Shearmen's hall and other places the which one Mr. Tomkys public preacher there did preach against, and the said preacher being present at the persuading reformation was there threatened and pushed at by certain lewd persons, but in the end it was reformed by the bailiffs'.*

In this way the contemporary chronicler of Shrewsbury described the beginning of a bitter dispute over the Shearmen's tree which raged between 1589 and 1591. The dispute arose from the custom of the Shearmen's or Clothworkers' company to mark their festival day on the first Sunday after Trinity (June 1 in 1589) by 'bringing in' an oak sapling from the countryside on the preceding day and setting it up before the door of the company hall - a medieval stone structure in Milk Street which stood beside the timber-framed mansion built by the draper George Proude in 1568. By the late 1580s some of the masters in the craft had been persuaded by Tomkys to seek the suppression of this practice. As the chronicler described, however, they met fierce resistance, and the disturbances which followed were only calmed by the intervention of the bailiffs, the two most senior officers in the town. But trouble broke out again at the festival in 1590. A proclamation on the Statute of Rebellion, warning of the consequences of breaching the Queen's peace, was read out to a large crowd which had gathered by the hall to see who was going to win - the party that wanted the tree

Shearmen's Hall and Proude's Mansion

'up', or the other that wanted it *'cast down'*. Over five hundred people were said to be present, representing one tenth of the town's population.

After this the authorities were determined to stifle further disorder. In 1591 on the day before the festival (5 June), they persuaded the craft masters to cancel the custom that year, and to prohibit any of the apprentices or journeymen from

Castle Hill in 1779

fetching in their tree. Among some of the younger clothworkers this order was greeted with disgust. Six in particular, led by the apprentice Richard Fernes, openly broadcast their opposition in the streets. At about 9 o'clock that night they left Shrewsbury through the Castle Gate, returning in the early hours of Sunday morning with a sapling cut from a copse in Alkmond park near Berwick. Scratching around the scrub at the foot of the castle hill, they penetrated the wall through the unguarded postern gate at St. Mary Waterlode, and transported the tree up the lane and through the streets to their hall where it was tied to one of the buttresses. By now the watch had been alerted. The junior bailiff Thomas Burnell was raised from his bed, and escorted to the hall. With the help of his officers, the hall door behind which the shearmen had locked themselves was smashed down and the lads arrested.

The next two months witnessed an intense psychological battle between the shearmen and the Shrewsbury magistrates. Two of the clothworkers confessed their errors, and after submitting themselves on petition to the correction of the bailiffs were released. The others, however, refused to explain their

behaviour or to admit that they had done anything wrong. Their sullen refusal to co-operate put the authorities in a corner. Neither side could now back down without a humiliating loss of face. On 12 June the four prisoners were indicted (charged) for unlawful assembly and riot. In addition, Richard Fernes was indicted for speaking these allegedly seditious words: *'Well Master Bailiff, I trust within these twelve years that I shall see the tree brought into this town of Salop in as solemn order as it ever was. And that neither bailiff nor any other person within the same town shall gainsay the same'.*

Although Fernes was separately sent for trial on the charge of sedition, his plea of not guilty was accepted by the trial jury and he was acquitted. In contrast, no further proceedings were taken on the indictments against all four men for unlawful assembly and riot because they were able, clearly with outside help, to obtain a writ of *habeas corpus* from the court of Queen's Bench at Westminster. That ensured that the case against them would have to be removed from Shrewsbury to a superior court. After hastily gathering support from some of the Shropshire gentry, the bailiffs, accompanied by the common sergeant, the town clerk and legal counsel, transported the shearmen to Warwick to appear before the assize judges on the Midland circuit. The shearmen were then bound over on 26 July to appear at the next Shrewsbury sessions (the court dealing with criminal matters) to be held on 23 August. There, while reserving a claim to their company's customs, they at last formally submitted and were *'quit for their disobedience'*. The whole matter was then referred to the arbitration of the town's recorder, or chief legal adviser, Thomas Owen of Condover, then a leading barrister. In due course Owen ordered that *'the usual tree should be used as heretofore have been, so it be done civilly and in loving order without contention'*. Despite great mental pressure and seven weeks in prison, the shearmen had secured recognition of their customary tree.

The record of this celebrated incident, which had the town buzzing for weeks, touches on many aspects of everyday life in

Tudor Shrewsbury. We can use it as a key to describing some of these aspects in more detail. The first of these involves the regulation of time.

Curfew and the watch

Why did the shearmen leave town at about 9 o'clock in the evening? In summer that was an hour before the curfew. At 10 o'clock, as town orders of 1583-4 show, no-one except the watchmen was allowed on the streets without a good excuse. An order of 1527 shows that in winter the three main gates were closed at 8 p.m., although the wicket gates set within them were kept open for another hour. The innholders and victuallers who from All Saints (1 November) to Candlemas (2 February) had to keep a lantern shining before their doors from 6 p.m., were then expected to douse them. By the late sixteenth century curfew was signalled by the tolling of the great bell at St. Mary's,

The night crier

and advertised by the night crier whose job by 1599 was *'to cry and call through the town in the night, giving all people knowledge of the clocks, to take heed of doors and locks, of fire and candlelight and so bidding them all good night'*.

Since no-one yet had the use of watches, bells helped townsfolk to monitor the time. So too did mechanical clocks, first introduced into England in the late thirteenth century. Both St. Alkmund's and St. Chad's churches had clocks by the 1450s - in St. Chad's case equipped with chimes. The town paid wages to the clock keepers and sometimes gave money to the churchwardens to repair the mechanisms. In 1592 a clock was also set up on the guildhall in the Cornmarket (The Square), complete with phases of the moon.

Clocks and bells helped outsiders to leave town before the curfew. A typical routine perhaps was described by Richard Basford in 1584. Questioned about the theft of a horse, he said that he had come to town on a Friday at 11 a.m. from Poynton near High Ercall (where he was staying with his uncle), done some shopping, and then supped and gambled at an alehouse run by a shoemaker until 7 or 8 p.m. He then left Shrewsbury for home. For the magistrates there was a sensitive point here. Anyone who spirited stolen goods out of town in the period immediately before curfew could take advantage both of nightfall and of the virtual shutting up of the town. The bailiff John Dawes was victimized in this way in December 1584. Both his horses, with their saddles and bridles, were stolen from his Roushill stables between 7 and 8 p.m. The thieves gained two hours headway and could not be caught.

Prior to curfew the watchmen were sworn in, *'charged upon their oaths that if any person or persons did walk the streets at undue time or seasons in the night that they should know who they were and what their business was to walk so late'* (1585). When necessary, torches could be lit to enable the bailiffs to administer the oath in the dark (1520). Even before curfew struck the watch began to check those passing through the wicket gates, like the two shearmen turned back at the Welsh Gate in June 1575 between 9 and 10 p.m. They had hoped to get to Kingsland to destroy some enclosures erected on the town commons. Instead they had to find another way out through one of the smaller postern gates in the town walls, giving access to the pasture behind the walls, and cross the Severn by boat. Fernes and his colleagues probably escaped similar obstruction by leaving earlier. At least thirteen posterns existed (see key to map), and in 1451 keys to eight of them had been allotted to responsible townsmen; so it seems that by the 1570s these gates may have been supervised less carefully than before.

In Shrewsbury the watch was organized on the basis of a rota or 'turn'. The turns passed through the streets of each of the three wards (the Stone, Welsh and Castle wards) in a prescribed sequence, passing from house to house. The obligation was shared among the respective householders in each house or tenement. Widows who kept their own households had to find a substitute. In the first half of the sixteenth century three or four householders from each ward, supervised if possible by an alderman or common councillor, were expected to man the watch. By 1585 the watch was split into companies of three, equipped with a bill (a pole tipped with a pike and a hook) or a wooden staff. Few though would enjoy staying up all night, especially in a freezing winter - although in practice the watchmen would have spent most of the small hours gathered by the fire in the porters' lodges at the gates. Some, like John Browne, were downright lazy: about 1613 he was gaoled for abdicating his duties as watchman and allowing someone to pinch his bill. On the other hand householders could avoid a turn by finding a substitute, such as the labourer Hugh ap Jevan who in 1598 charged 3d or 4d to stand in as a watchman. His clients included a shoemaker and an embroiderer. The rate was not unreasonable. At that date it would buy about nine pints of beer, and a householder could expect four to seven turns a year.

For those who did enjoy watch-duty, it was exciting to accost shadowy figures in the dark, universally known as 'nightwalkers'. On 13 June 1585 the three watchmen for the Stone ward were patrolling the Cornmarket at midnight when they spotted a knot of nightwalkers in the High Street. The officers approached them shouting out *'who went there at that time of night'*, but got no reply. Further questioning was greeted with a sudden burst of abuse - *'rogues'*, *'threepenny knaves'* - provoking a fight in which a woman in the party claimed later to have been hit in the face by a bill and knocked to the ground. In the winter of 1634, two watchmen, a sawyer and a trowman, were baited by the clothier John Browne whom they met at Mardol Head at about 10 p.m. They asked him why he was still on the streets. *'The king's business'*, he replied sarcastically. In the subsequent struggle to arrest him, Browne used his yard, or wooden staff, to smash the trowman in the face.

Many incidents of this kind involved stragglers from the alehouses. Dealing with such people was undoubtedly the most fraught part of the watchman's job. As the snuffing of the innholders' and victuallers' lights indicates, drinking time in winter was meant to end at 9 p.m. Children seeking to earn a penny at that hour by singing at one of the many Shrewsbury alehouses could earn a rebuke from the alehouse keeper. *'It was no due time for singing, it being about 9 o'clock'*, as one put it in December 1625. In summer the taverns and alehouses could stay open until curfew at 10 p.m.

Watchman with bill

The preceding hour was especially troublesome as customers turned out into the streets, some inevitably the worse for drink. At that time we hear of drinkers throwing stones from the garrets in St. Mary's steeple; snatching a harp from a musician who had just been playing the alehouses and toying with it along the street; staggering home to swear at their wives *'to the disturbance of the neighbourhood';* or, like the butcher Richard Morris in 1616, *'cutting of window ropes, tumbling of block stones and timber trees overthwart the streets, rearing up pieces of timber to men's doors and breaking of stiles and gates in the way leading unto Meole Brace'*. Such behaviour was deeply resented since most people had already gone to bed. If it was a weekday they would have spent a long day at work, with an early rise next morning to come.

The daily rhythm

For most Salopians the day began much earlier than we are used to now. At 4 o'clock in the morning the daybell was tolled - *'to raise the workers'* as it was put in 1523 -

originally in St. Alkmund's, but from 1557 in St. Julian's. Before the Reformation this hour probably also coincided with the first celebration of mass or 'morrow mass', celebrated at St. George's chapel in St. Chad's. At the same time the watch stood down (recorded in 1521), the gates were re-opened, and the first residents began to appear on the streets. For most households one of the first tasks was to fetch water for domestic use. The earliest attempt to build

A water carrier

a conduit to supply the town did not start until 1555, after which water could be obtained from the conduit by filling distinctive tankards which held two to three gallons. Before then maidservants and other water carriers had to use wells or the river Severn. For fetching water and bringing clothes to the wash, residents at the bottom of Wyle Cop could take a short cut through the backyard of the Higgons family to a small door set high up on the town wall. A ladder led down to a plank placed over the ditch at the base, from where a path led through the Grey Friars to the river. While the water carriers were busy, shutters were opened and shops prepared for the first customers, although many tradesmen rented shops away from their own residence and first had to walk to their place of work.

The length of the working day varied from trade to trade. The Weavers' company permitted its masters to work from 4 a.m. to 9 p.m., while the cloth merchants and the shearmen agreed in 1580 that apprentices and journeymen could only be set to work between 4 a.m. and 8 p.m. But these were maximum limits. In practice the situation in Shrewsbury was no doubt similar to that described in other towns. Although some trades like the blacksmiths and butchers were renowned for starting as early as possible, most craftsmen were content to begin at about 6 o'clock in the morning. This was reflected by the fact that labourers who wished to be hired for a day's work had to gather with their tools at a central location between about 5 and 6 a.m. From 1559 6 o'clock was also marked by the ringing of a bell in St. Julian's church. Drapers wanting to ride to the Monday cloth market at Oswestry could not leave before this bell had tolled. In the late sixteenth century that was also the hour when the parishioners of St. Mary's sent their children to church for Sunday catechism.

It was normal to work for a few hours before taking breakfast at about 9 a.m. A 1495 statute allowed half an hour for breakfast, an hour for 'dinner', which was taken at about midday, and another half an hour for a light meal in the afternoon. Between mid May and mid August the dinner break could be extended by another thirty minutes for a siesta. Otherwise work continued to at least 6 p.m. and often later. St. Julian's bell - known as Hallywell's knell after John Hallywell, a parishioner and one of the bailiffs in 1558-9 - was rung at 4 a.m., 6 a.m., noon and 6 p.m., and so marked out most of the principal divisions of the day. These were the arrangements on weekdays. On Saturday, when wages were paid to labourers and the journeymen, work ended earlier. The Shrewsbury weavers were expected to lay down the shuttle at midday - extended to 4 p.m. in about 1588 - although they could lay in marks on the loom. Sunday, of course, was largely a rest day. The Mercers' company would only allow shop doors or windows to be opened on Sunday to cater for special requests. Sabbatarianism, or the strict observance of Sunday as a day of rest, became a powerful ideal of English protestantism, and many of the Shrewsbury craft fellowships passed ordinances after the Reformation strictly prohibiting any work on that day. But these measures were meant to ensure that people took their religious duties more seriously, and were not new in themselves. The Barbers' company, for instance, had forbidden Sunday shaving, in private or in public, since at least 1432.

Apart from Saturdays and Sundays then, and feast days, the opportunities for recreation were restricted to only two or three hours before curfew. Many went early to bed. Court records in 1564 reveal a carpenter heading home for bed at 7 p.m., and others trying to sleep by eight. In 1586 several of the town councillors served with a summons to an election on the next day were already in bed by 8 or 9 p.m. For them it was the end of a long working day of 12 to 14 hours in length. Within another eight hours the daybell would sound again and the daily cycle would begin anew.

The Salopian calendar

Life was not all toil. It has been calculated that before the Reformation a third of the year could in theory have been taken off from work, if Sundays and Saints' days are added together.

Even afterwards many workers continued to take holidays on some of these feast days and during the parish wakes, much to the disgust of the puritans. Together with the main Christmas, Easter and Whitsun holidays, these could still amount to four or more weeks a year. The craft fellowships also had their own festivals to look forward to. In the late fifteenth century the Shearmen's company marked their festival by laying on a meal of cheese, saffron cakes and ale, consumed in a hall strewn with rushes, and accompanied by the music of the waits (minstrels employed by the corporation). A century later the arrangements had changed little. The hall was now decorated with flowers and a bottle of wine was usually bought for the masters' wives. Attendance was compulsory. On the preceding day when the tree was fetched in by the apprentices and younger masters, drums were beaten and gunpowder exploded. Townspeople lived in remembrance of such festivals and in expectation of the next. Before the Reformation the Salopian calendar was rich in such anticipations. In the description that follows, the calendar is described mainly as it was before the Reformation began to cut away some of these traditional customs.

One way to describe the calendar is by its seasonal divisions. In towns Candlemas (2 February) marked the notional beginning of the year. It was then, in Shrewsbury as elsewhere, that the town commons normally reverted to private hands for rent, and the winter lighting arrangements came to an end. In due course May Day was traditionally accepted as the start of summer. Certainly at Shrewsbury the town waits, whose playing emphasized the seasonal framework, were hired about that time. Autumn began at Michaelmas when the commons were thrown open again and, in the fifteenth century at least, the times for the watch were re-set. Finally, judging from lighting regulations, deep winter was thought to run from All Saints' day (1 November) to Candlemas.

Cutting across this seasonal calendar, however, was another based upon the liturgical year of the church. We can see its influence in the dates of the 'scarlet days' appointed in 1569, when the aldermen and common councillors were expected to wait upon the bailiffs in their best gowns and accompany them to church. These were held on Christmas day, New Year's day (the feast of the Circumcision), Candlemas, Easter day, Whitsun, the Sunday after the civic elections held at the start of October, and All Saints' day. Before the Reformation another scarlet day would have been held at Corpus Christi, while the bailiffs and their colleagues might also share a meal or a drinking on Epiphany, Ascension day, Trinity Sunday, and at the end of the fasts on the eve of the feasts of St. John the Baptist (24 June), Saints Peter and Paul (29 June) and the translation of St. Thomas Becket (7 July). Of these occasions only the post-election gathering was not linked to a feast day. This liturgical calendar was, and still is, at its most elaborate in the six months between Christmas and the summer feast of Corpus Christi, during which all the major observances of Christianity occur. The same period also saw an equally rich concentration of ceremonies and popular customs, of which the fetching in of the Shearmen's tree was but one example.

The period began at Christmas, the start of a holiday lasting for the twelve days until Epiphany. Weekly receipts of tolls taken at the gates show a steep decline in commercial traffic at this time. Like today, Christmas was marked by the giving of presents, and there was obviously something of a pre-Christmas shopping rush. Leather products, gloves in particular, made popular gifts. In 1564 the glover Robert Gyttyns claimed in a law suit that David ap Griffith had agreed at Mardol Head to work for him in the fortnight before Christmas, but had failed to do so. Gyttyns had already released another journeyman who had been working for him, and so suddenly found himself unable to meet demand. Not only had he lost many customers, *but also the taking of much money against Christmas for want of having wares ready made'.*

Traditionally Christmas was also a time for fooling about and momentarily reversing the pretensions of authority. This was the function of the 'mummers', 'lords of misrule', and 'boy

St. George's mummers

bishops' (known at Ludlow and Hereford). Mummers were men, usually in masked disguise, who knocked on the doors of the inhabitants and enacted a folk drama: the legend of St. George was particularly popular. At the same time they might subject the more prominent citizens, such as the aldermen, to playful criticism, ideally receiving some drink in return. Although the parishioners of St. Mary's were asked in 1585 to report Christmas mummers and lords of misrule to their own church court, there is no direct evidence of their presence in Shrewsbury. We are better informed about the breakfast which the bailiffs laid on at their expense between Matins and High Mass on Christmas day. In 1523 these breakfasts were temporarily abandoned *'for diverse considerations and misorder'.* Perhaps this was due to the kind of problems encountered at Ludlow by 1545. There so many people had taken advantage of this customary hospitality that the costs to the bailiffs threatened to get out of hand. In Shrewsbury at least, less generous breakfasts had been reinstated by 1547. The bailiffs now met only with their 'equals', and sometimes received a small allowance from the town stock, although the poet Thomas Churchyard later boasted that the town was noted for its Christmas feasting which *'... compares with all I know/Save London sure, whose state is far more'.*

During the holiday the bailiffs also had the option to employ the waits to play for them every morning, dressed in orange coats.

After Christmas and the feasts of Epiphany and Candlemas (celebrated with a blaze of tapers in the churches), attention turned towards Lent. In Shrewsbury, as elsewhere, the apprentices and other youngsters marked Shrove Tuesday with vigorous games of football, although most of our evidence comes from the late sixteenth century when the authorities tried to suppress them. On that day, for instance, the shearman John Gyttyns junior once petulantly threw the ball away after being asked by the sergeant to hand it over to him. He was imprisoned until he apologized. Lent itself began on the next day (Ash Wednesday) when the prohibitions against marriages and meat eating came into force. As early as 1295 grants of tolls to the town mentioned lampreys for sale before Easter; and the receipts of stallage - a toll paid for pitching stalls in the markets, including the fish market - show a distinct peak during Lent, which may indicate increased sales of fish at that time. Some transactions were substantial. In 1563 the merchant Robert Ireland sued the shoemaker Richard Wright for money owed for the sale on 19 February of thirteen *'couples of salt fish'* and 150 stock (dried) fish for £4 9s 0d. Ireland was obviously selling wholesale, but smaller retail sales of fish in Lent are also recorded. Lent observance was taken seriously. In 1568 the gentleman John Leighton sued Ralph Phellypes for defamation, claiming that the defendant had accused him of eating three stolen pigs during Lent in a saddler's house (probably an alehouse), contrary to the laws of the land. When the public preacher John Tomkys fell terminally ill in the winter of 1591-2, he had to obtain special licence to eat flesh in Lent to rebuild his strength; and nine butchers were also charged with slaughtering meat during Lent in 1609.

Lent passed into the great drama of Holy week and Easter day, during which the bellringers of St. Mary's were traditionally rewarded with two calves' heads for their efforts. Afterwards the town enjoyed the Easter holidays. Like Christmas, and Whitsuntide too, this period also saw a decline in market traffic at the gates. From then on, with the approach of summer, the tempo of ceremonial and customary activity increased sharply. May Day eve, traditionally a time for courting games, was naturally observed in Shrewsbury. In 1549, according to the town chronicler, *'This year and the Tuesday after Easter holidays* [May day eve that year] *2 young men of Salop whose names were Edmund Reynolds and Robert Clarke were smothered under the castle hill, hiding themselves from maids, the hill falling part thereof upon them'*. Coincidentally, this was one of those rare moments when May Day eve coincided with Hock Tuesday, the first Tuesday after Easter, when the roles of the sexes were ritually reversed by such practices as the 'heaving' of the men-folk - a widespread custom in the Midlands. It is just possible that the two men were hiding from the girls to avoid that fate, although Hocktide customs normally involved wives and husbands.

Such ritual inversions were typical of early summer. From the 1520s until about 1552 the town sometimes contributed to the expenses of a folk play involving a lord of misrule known as the

Abbot of Marham or Marall or Mayvoll - probably a nonsense name. For several years the part of the Abbot was played by Richard Glasier. Dressed up in a special robe and sandals, he paraded through the streets in May time, escorted by the minstrels and preceded by the town crier shouting out for all to attend upon the Abbot. The authorities took such ridicule in good part. As the bailiffs' accounts show, they were quite happy to help sponsor the Abbot themselves. Local gentry too turned a blind eye to invasions of their property when townsmen came out to chop down trees for their maypoles. In 1591 the Shearmen's tree was cut from a copse owned by Sir Edmund Lucy, lord of Berwick manor, which he leased to a Shrewsbury draper. In the unusual circumstances of that year, however, there was some doubt

The maypole

if Lucy really had shown no objection. Other entertainments were also laid on during May 'for the enjoyment of the town', including the provision of music and drama, such as the Robin Hood play put on in 1553. Although summer mummers and lords of misrule were again frowned upon by the public preacher in 1585, a lord of misrule was still active in May 1619. Maying in fact could extend into June, and maypoles were still being brought into town as late as Midsummer day.

Much of this period overlapped with the moveable feasts of Rogationtide, Ascension and Whitsun. The first was always associated with the universal practice of beating the parish boundaries, known in St. Julian's parish as 'bannering'. In the larger parishes of St. Mary and St. Chad, which took in extensive rural areas, it was impractical to attempt a complete perambulation. Instead the parishioners probably met at selected sites of topographical importance. One such site in St. Chad's parish may have been Cadogan's Cross, selected in 1543 for a rogation sermon preached by the chaplain of the Lord President of the Council in the Marches. The cross stood beyond Frankwell by an ancient chapel and hermitage on what is now known as The Mount, adjacent to one of the town bars. These were wooden barriers placed across the road which, like the bars beside the Severn at Coton, marked the entrance to the suburbs. In times of danger, as in 1461 during the Wars of the Roses, they could be strung with chains. Rogationtide was noted for its public sermons. Among the preachers rewarded by the town on these occasions were the Dominican or 'preaching' friars.

After Rogation and Ascension came Whitsuntide, famous for its religious plays. These were usually staged in a semicircular amphitheatre called the 'dry quarry' near the Austin Friars - not to be confused with the 'wet quarry', known today as The Dingle. The site (now occupied by the swimming pool) was used for digging clay as well as for wrestling, bull-baiting, cock fighting and other pastimes. The plays themselves were quite expensive to put on, and all the craft fellowships were expected to contribute to their production. Money was spent on bells, gold foil, false beards, silver and gold paper, gunpowder, and painted scenery. Dramas included the martyrdom of Saints Feliciane and Sabine in 1516, which was watched by the abbot of Shrewsbury, and the Kings of Cologne, i.e. the Magi of Epiphany, in 1518. The plays probably reached their greatest fame when Thomas Ashton, headmaster of the grammar school, revived them in the 1560s. He himself was *'chief actor'* in the plays which *'lasted all the holidays'* in 1569. Before their final disappearence, perhaps as a result of stronger protestant scruples, the Whitsun plays were very popular, and people travelled some distance to see them. The London haberdasher John Smith, for example, who was visiting friends in Leominster, travelled up to see the plays in 1569. Notable spectators at other times included in 1446 Lady Talbot, wife of the Earl of Shrewsbury who was killed fighting the French at Castillon near Bordeaux in 1453; the Prince of Wales in 1493 and 1495; the Lord President of the Council in the Marches in 1533, who sat with the bailiffs in a special viewing box; and other *'noblemen'* in 1569.

Carrying the monstrance in Corpus Christi procession, 15th century

Within ten days of the Whitsun holiday came the great feast days of Trinity Sunday and Corpus Christi. Since their guild was dedicated to the Trinity, the former was especially important to the Drapers' company. Every year they bought tapers for their altar in St. Mary's towards that day. But it was Corpus Christi, the following Thursday, which represented the pinnacle of the civic year. This feast had first been celebrated in England in the early fourteenth century and was commonly marked by great processions. In Shrewsbury the procession was made up of the craft fellowships or 'companies', dressed in special livery and bearing their banners and tapers through the town. The victuallers led the way, followed by most of the leather, metal and wood-working crafts. After them came the textile workers, then the Glovers' and Tailors' companies, and finally the prestigious Mercers' and Drapers' companies. Behind them, carried beneath a splendid canopy in a transparent vessel or 'monstrance', came the host - the wafer of consecrated bread that was Christ's flesh. There is no direct evidence for the route of the procession, but it probably connected the Abbey Foregate - a separate jurisdiction until 1586 - with the town, and at some stage may have wound its way around St. Mary's churchyard. When they were not quarrelling over the disputed Merivale area on the abbey side of the Stone Bridge, the abbot and his associates usually sat down at Corpus Christi with the principal townsmen for a drinking.

After all the ritual inversions of early summer, the procession displayed Salopian society once more in one of its official guises - as a united hierarchy of male craftsmen. Not only did the masters and journeymen line up in order of their seniority in each craft, but the order of the procession itself was carefully worked out. A big dispute over precedence broke out in 1461 between the Carpenters and the combined fellowship of Fletchers, Bowyers and Coopers. A detailed agreement was drawn up to satisfy both sides, describing how the masters in each company should be paired off and in what position their banners and those of the journeymen should be carried. All the craft fellowships emphasized the ideal of public unity by insisting on compulsory attendance. For the merchants this posed a problem since Corpus Christi coincided with the great Coventry fair. The Mercers allowed their masters to visit the fair provided they first obtained permission to be absent.

Christ's body symbolized Christian fellowship. Corpus Christi then was also a time for at least trying to pretend that you lived in amity with your colleagues and neighbours. The Drapers' records show something of the spirit of the occasion. They decorated their hall with herbs, and purchased bread, ale and cheese for the taper bearers. They also held a breakfast before the procession, and a company drinking afterwards at one of the taverns like the Gullet (on the site of the present Hole In The Wall pub), where they were entertained by minstrels, such as the Earl of Shrewsbury's in 1504.

Covered way from the Sextry to St. Chad's

The pivotal role of Corpus Christi in the Salopian calendar is shown by the way in which many companies grouped their most important meetings around it. Take 1525 as an example, when the feast day fell on 15 June. The Saddlers held their elections on 16 June, the Glovers and the Weavers on Sunday 18 June, the Mercers on 19 June, and the Carpenters on 25 June. The Barbers probably held their elections on Corpus Christi itself. In addition, on the 18th the Shearmen celebrated their festival, while the Tailors and Skinners in their best gowns held another procession, escorting their candle to the shrine of St. Winifred in the abbey. On the next day they audited their accounts and sat down to a company dinner. The Drapers too sometimes met for a drinking on the Sunday after Corpus Christi. In 1502, for example, they spent 4s 2d on wine, wafers and apples at the Sextry tavern, a famous establishment (on the site of the present Golden Cross pub), which was connected to St. Chad's by a covered way passing over Kiln Lane (Princess Street) to the churchyard. The Sextry had been granted to the Mercers' company in 1467, and every Friday their tenant had to pay one penny from the rent to each inmate in St. Chad's almshouses.

Two more important festivals were still to come. Both the vigils of St. John the Baptist (the eve of 24 June - Midsummer day) and Saints Peter and Paul (the eve of 29 June) had once been celebrated by great civic drinkings, as in 1442 when over eleven gallons of wine were consumed by the bailiffs and their colleagues on Midsummer eve. Minstrels and trumpeters were also rewarded on these occasions. By the 1510s these drinkings were no longer recorded, although the Drapers' records show that Midsummer eve continued to be marked by the traditional marching watch until 1508 at least. Pitch was bought and placed in a metal basin mounted on a pole, known as a cresset. This was then lit and carried through the streets in a 'triumph', with the bailiffs leading the way. In 1483 the company had 46 torches in stock which were probably kept for that occasion. Once again the fellowship sat down to a drinking and a meal, typically of saffron cakes and cheese. All the other companies

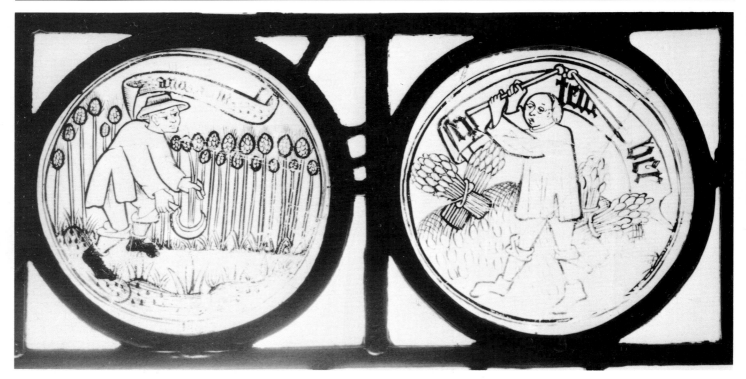

Harvesting (from Lower Pulley farm)

would have had similar arrangements, and the sight of hundreds of flickering torches being carried through Shrewsbury on a summer night must have been spectacular.

With the end of June the principal period of civic ritual came to an end. Although several important feast days were yet to be celebrated in the six months before Christmas, there were fewer occasions for public festivity. The onset of harvest in particular required attention of a more down-to-earth kind. In 1577 journeymen sawyers were allowed to look for work in the fields during the harvest provided they first obtained permission from their wardens in the Carpenters' company.

Otherwise only Election night, described in chapter 2, and All Saints' day disturbed the more routine character of the calendar. On the latter occasion the streets were first cleared of timber and rubbish. Craftsmen then played football in the pasture behind the walls, while the bailiffs and their assistants enjoyed another drinking and strolled from street to street meeting the residents, a tradition still kept in 1552. By 1588 the male householders or 'streeters' of Doglane (Claremont Street) were complaining that this *'laudable custom'* was no longer observed. Their lament illustrated the emptier calendar which appeared after the Reformation had undermined many of the customs we have just described (see chapter 9).

Chapter 2 - Authority

Petitions and Submission

After their arrest for fetching in the tree in 1591, the six shearmen were expected to apologize. To do this a standard procedure had to be followed. A submission was drawn up on a piece of paper addressed to the bailiffs, in which offenders admitted that they had behaved badly and said that they were sorry. These submissions, which could relate to a variety of minor offences, comprised one of three types of petition. The other two included, first, petitions which sought a favour of some kind - for example, to be admitted as a burgess, to be granted a plot of corporation land, to receive money from one of the town charities, or to be appointed to one of the minor civic offices like the common gaoler. Secondly, there were petitions which sought redress for a particular grievance. This might involve a reeking dung heap, a blocked lane, a filthy pig-sty, a snapping dog, an abusive neighbour, a 'scolding' wife, or a surly servant. A petition in 1594 from the brewer Humphrey Baynes illustrates this type. Baynes claimed that on 9 July, intending to make a delivery of beer in town, he had instructed his servant Richard Clarke to harness his dray horse to the cart. But when he came to inspect the 'gear' (harness), he found that it had been attached in the wrong way, and that the horse could have been badly hurt. He stepped into the brewhouse and told Clarke to fix the harness properly, but his servant snapped back that he could do it himself. When Baynes strode up to correct him, Clarke shoved his master up against the wall, pushed him round the room, then dragged him outside and threw him over the back of the cart. Baynes's ankle was so badly injured that he now had to use a stick to get about. He petitioned the bailiffs to summon Clarke and punish him according to the statute, *'as well for his better amendment therein as also that it may be an example to other of his fellows who otherwise will be ready to do the like'*.

Such petitions show how readily Salopians looked to the bailiffs to resolve domestic or neighbourly disputes. Submissive petitions, by contrast, illustrate another way in which respect for authority was acknowledged.

The Bailiffs, 1590s

Petitioners were treated rather like insolent schoolboys. If they said they were sorry, they would be released from prison and the matter forgotten. But first they had to make an abject apology. A typical example, from 1598, also involved Richard Fernes. Since the incident involving the Shearmen's tree in 1591, there had obviously been bad feeling between Fernes and Thomas Burnell, the junior bailiff whom Fernes had confronted on that occasion in the company hall. In 1597 Burnell was again elected as one of the two bailiffs for the civic year 1597-8, this time as the 'high' or senior bailiff. On Sunday 18 June 1598 the Shearmen held their festival day, and it is clear that either then, or on the preceding day, when the tree was fetched in, a row took place between the two men during which Fernes roundly abused the bailiff. The circumstances are unclear: perhaps Burnell had sought to ban the tree again, or to restrict the festivities. At any rate, Fernes was arrested and thrown into gaol. On Monday he put in his petition:

> '*Humbly submitteth himself unto your worship your orator Richard Fernes, now remaining in ward by your commitment with Roger Phelips one of the sergeants of mace of the said town, for speaking indecent words and not obeying your worship's commandment which he confesseth to deserve greater punishment but for that he is heartily sorry for his said offence and hopeth to be restored to his former liberty, and this for god's love. 19 June 1598. Your worship's prisoner,* [signed] *Richard Fernes*'.

Insulting figures of authority, such as the public preacher, craft wardens, night watchmen or other civic officers, often led to imprisonment and the need to apologize in this way. More usually, however, imprisonment occurred not because of the offence itself, but for failing to pay the subsequent fine. These fines were imposed by the Great Court, and covered such offences as breaches of market regulations, assaults and public nuisances. Drink was involved in many such cases. Of 91 petitions received from 99 prisoners in 1612-13, 24 involved boozing after curfew, and several others related to

drunken behaviour. Petitioners usually stated that they were poor and had found it difficult to pay the fines in question; or that imprisonment prevented them from supporting their families. In 1571 the glover Nicholas Low was imprisoned for being drunk during a service in St. Julian's church. He begged to be released because he had a wife and several children who relied upon his '*gains*' to survive.

The wording of Fernes's petition was typical, and can be found in examples throughout the Tudor period. Petitioners often described themselves as '*orators*', i.e. as those who would pray for the persons petitioned, and ended with the phrase '*and this for god's love*'. Handwriting and the use of set phrases tells us that most petitions must have been drawn up by scribes employed for that purpose. This was necessary partly because so few petitioners could write. Of the 99 prisoners who petitioned in 1612-13, for example, only 29 could sign their names. In fact we know that many petitions were drawn up by attorneys working in the Small Court which dealt with civil litigation. In 1591 one of these attorneys, John Benion, was described as the '*common supplicant*', and it seems to have been his job to present the petitions to the bailiffs.

Petitions in fact made up part of a formal procedure for dealing with minor offences. Take the case of the servant Thomas Lightbound in 1611. First, the offence: while drunk in his master's house, he had bawled out to his mistress and her daughter, '*God's wound, give me my supper*'. Second: for his swearing and insubordination he was thrown into the Welsh Gate prison. Third: he put in a formal petition and apologized. Fourth: he was then released. In this sequence, a petition containing an apology cleared the slate as if the offence had never occurred. What people found unsettling was a refusal to apologize. In such cases the act of insubordination remained uncleared. In a small community, this was a very troubling experience. In the case of the Shearmen's tree, as we have seen, it lent an edge of hysteria to the magistrates' reaction.

'Michaelmas gents'

Petitions were always sent to the two bailiffs. They were elected each year on the Friday after Michaelmas (29 September), together with six sessors (assistants), two coroners and the common sergeant. Six auditors were also elected on the Thursday before Michaelmas. They were responsible for checking the bailiffs' accounts and the chamberlain's supervision of the town stock. The coroners held inquests in cases of sudden death, and drew up lists of jurymen for the sessions (see chapter 8). But their main task was to supervise expenditure on the upkeep of the town fabric including the bridges, the gates, and the great circuit of walls erected in the thirteenth century. The common sergeant was assisted by two other sergeants, chosen by each incoming bailiff. Each sergeant was responsible for a ward, and their job was to issue writs, oversee arrests and collect fines, for which they kept their own accounts. Since 1445 an elaborate system of rules had been in place to ensure that no-one monopolized the principal offices. Bailiffs, sessors and coroners, for example, could not be re-elected within three years after leaving office. Until the 1560s, when arrangements became more flexible, the senior or 'high' bailiff was nearly always chosen from among the twelve aldermen, while the junior or 'low' bailiff might be either an alderman or one of the 24 common councillors. Together, these two bodies comprised the borough council, the effective governing body of the town.

During the Tudor period the office of bailiff was dominated by drapers, mercers and wool merchants. In the sixteenth century, for example, they provided two-thirds of the 200 men elected to that post. Most of the others were lawyers or town gentry; only a tiny number came from other trades. The reason for this was simple. Since 1389 all bailiffs had to be worth at least £100 in goods, or possess property worth £10 a year. It was essential too that they had sufficient resources to support the dignity or 'worship' of their office. Only the richer trades could provide men able to fulfil these conditions, and the merchants were by far the wealthiest body of men in Shrewsbury.

In the great 'subsidy' or tax of 1525, for example, they paid three times as much per head as any other occupational group in the town. In normal circumstances then, it was hard for Salopians to imagine how anyone other than the rich could rule.

Marks of deference reinforced the bailiffs' authority. In their presence Salopians had to doff their caps or hats and address them with the formal 'you' or 'ye' rather than with the more familiar 'thou'. In return bailiffs were expected to be even-handed and to show a good moral example. The ideal was represented by men like Roger Thornes, seven times bailiff between 1497 and 1530.

Thornes arms

He was of gentry stock with a country residence at Shelvock and a town house at Thornes Place near the famous Raven inn in High Pavement (Castle Street, on the site of Woolworth's). Later on, about 1625, his descendants built a mansion on the other side of the street, known as Thornes Hall, which was demolished in 1921 to make way for the Co-op building. Roger himself was called 'The Wise Thornes' for his expert guidance on town affairs and for the personal advice he dispensed to town and country-folk alike. Then there was the mercer Roger Luter, elected bailiff in 1543, 1551 and 1562. When he died in 1601 in his nineties, it was said of him that;

'he was a gentleman of small lands, yet by his wisdom, countenance and wise government bore it out with such credit that twice his betters did not bear the like port of humanity'.

Not all bailiffs were so well regarded. In 1610 James Barker got in trouble for standing with his hat on before the bailiffs and 'thou-ing' bailiff Jones. Prominent citizens could be scornful too. When Alderman Thomas Stury got involved in a row with Bailiff Owen in 1576 he jammed his cap down over his eye-brows. *'I am your bailiff'*, said Owen. *'Yea'*, replied Stury, *'you are my bailiff for this year'*. *'I will be a good fellow the next year'*, Owen went on. *'Then I will talk with you'*, answered Stury. The exchange shows that bailiffs could not expect automatic respect. In a small community their personalities and failings would have been familiar to many. Some perhaps were known to be hard masters or creditors; others to flaunt their wealth. Rich men should be modest. As an irate farmer told a young Thomas Burnell in 1565, when he came out to Welbatch to buy six sheep, he might make *'a jolly show'* in his shop of his wealth, but he was no better *'than a rook of the castle'*. Why defer to such men simply because they had been elected bailiff for a year? As Barker put it, *'he would be as good a man as Mr. Bailiff Jones after Michaelmas'*. The bailiffs in fact were often described sarcastically as *'Michaelmas gents'*. The butcher Richard Beddowe expressed it bluntly in 1615, reviling the bailiff and apothecary Roger Blakeway as;

'hodge hodge [slang for cretin] and hoddy doddy [cuckold], and a Michaelmas gent, and one that fell out of a crow's nest; and did bid a turd for him and a fart for him, and threaten him that he would be meet with him after Michaelmas, and that he was a better man than Mr. Bailiff'.

Council and Commons

The aldermen and common councillors usually gathered for business about ten to twenty times each year, although the aldermen sometimes met separately. Meetings were held in the Council Chamber which formed part of an interesting collection of buildings in the Cornmarket. If about 1550 you had stood at the site of the Market Hall (not built until 1596), and looked towards the High Street, you would have seen half way down on the right a stone tower erected in 1451-2, called the Exchequer or 'treasure house', where the town records and money chest were kept. It had small glass windows (smashed by juvenile hooligans in 1523), and a chamber in which votes were taken during council elections. Beside the tower was a two-storey building. The ground floor was occupied by shops, while the upper floor was an open hall - the Council Chamber itself - connected to the Exchequer tower by an inner door.

The Guildhall and Exchequer

At right angles to this building, blocking much of the High Street end, was the Guildhall, often called the Booth Hall. At ground level were more shops and above was another hall which was used for court business, parliamentary elections and meetings of the burgesses or 'Commons'. At the 'nether' or lower end it also contained a chamber which until 1574, when it began to be used as a jury and meeting room, was available for rent. Like the Council Chamber, the Guildhall was reached by stairs from the Cornmarket. Both halls were also equipped with urinal tubs in 1522.

The whole complex had originally been erected in 1310-11, but extensions and refurbishments were undertaken in the 1450s and in 1547. In 1578, the Council Chamber was also *'beautified'* with wainscot, glass windows and a chimney, and a ceiling was inserted. It was then optimistically named the 'Chamber of Concord'. In 1741-2 this part, also called the Green Room, was altered again and fashionable sash windows were inserted (see illustration). The Guildhall itself was wainscotted and ceiled over in 1583-4 and a new set of winding stairs was erected, enclosed within a timber frame. Unfortunately one of the building labourers, a *'bold strong man'* named William Eyton, fell from the scaffolding to his death; he was buried in St. Chad's churchyard where he had often worked as a grave digger.

The borough council co-opted its own members. The aldermen chose replacements from the common councillors; and they in turn from the Commons whom they were supposed to represent. There was always competition to become a councillor. Sitting members naturally schemed to get their relations and cronies elected. In 1517, for example, Alderman Thomas Trentham junior was accused of manipulating council and other elections, *'contrary to the will and minds of the well disposed men being craft men within the said town'*. But he was not always successful. As the shearman William Pickering put it, *'some time he hath sped* [succeeded] *and some time not'*. After 1560, however, election disputes became more common and bitter. There were two reasons for this. First, councillors were serving for a longer period than before. Secondly, the number of wealthy aspirants to office increased sharply: male membership of the Drapers' and Mercers' companies, for example, rose from 76 masters in 1525 to 122 in 1587. More merchants than ever before were chasing the limited

number of places that became available. In such conditions bribery and corruption flourished. Disputes took place throughout the 1560s, 1570s and 1580s, with parties taking their grievances to the court of Star Chamber at Westminster, or seeking arbitration from the Council in the Marches. In 1568 it was said that every time a vacancy arose, councillors were desperately promised money loans or leases of property to get their votes. During one such dispute in 1571 Thomas Ashton, headmaster of the grammar school, lashed out at the parties in a sermon, complaining that *'it was a shame to bring such a stink of their factions and debates'*. One of the worst offenders was Alderman Thomas Sherer whose son probably built Sherer's Mansion at the bottom of the Wyle Cop (on the site of the present N.C.P. carpark). In 1587 he was described as *'the very bellows that kindleth the fire of all these discords'*, with a *'greedy appetite to establish a strong faction and sovereignty to himself'*.

Two particular tactics were often used in council disputes. One was to accuse an opposing councillor of living outside the town or its rural liberties, which was forbidden. In 1572, for example, an attempt was made to eject the merchant Robert Ireland senior from the aldermanic bench for residing at Lythwood outside the liberties. It was said that he no longer attended Easter communion, and had stopped contributing to his parish or to the watch. His children, it was claimed, were sent to school in Shrewsbury with their meals ready-made, and returned to Lythwood after a couple of days, or at most at the end of the week. The second tactic was to exploit the twenty days rule. Whenever a vacancy on the council arose, a new election was supposed to be held within twenty days. But if the bailiffs could be won over, the summons for the election could either be issued immediately (one in 1586 was for 7 a.m. on the morning after an alderman had died); or postponed until after the twenty days. In each case the aim of such *'sinister labour, devises and practices'*, as they were described in 1568, was to hold the vote when opponents would not be able to attend. At its worst, council faction was felt to eat away at the fabric of community relations. In 1587, after one such dispute had been settled, a banquet was

Sherer's Mansion

held and the church bells rung *'to the great rejoicing of the Commons'*. But their joy was premature. Similar problems continued into the seventeenth century. It was not until the town council was doubled in size in 1638 that the situation improved.

Although town business was decided by the aldermen and common councillors, most of their agreements had to be approved by the Commons (i.e. the burgesses or freemen) who, together with the bailiffs and council, formed the *communitas* or corporation of Shrewsbury. Approval was usually a formality. The Commons would be summoned to an assembly in the Guildhall, and through a 'speaker' give their assent to council motions. But their role was not completely nominal. Sometimes minor petitions were left to the Commons to deal with; and occasionally they even put their foot down, objecting to proposed leases of corporation property.

The privileges of the burgesses included freedom to trade exempt from tolls; prior access to the town mill on the Stone Bridge to grind their corn when water levels were low; the sole right to retail ale outside fair time (although this was impossible to enforce); redemption from the cattle pound for half the normal price; the choice of auditors and Shrewsbury's two members of parliament; and, after 1552, cheap-rate admission for their sons to the grammar school for 4d. They also had the right to graze their cows for a fee on Kingsland and in the pasture behind the walls (which included the present Quarry park). Access to Kingsland, nominally rented from the Crown, was available from Michaelmas (29 September) until Candlemas (2 February): in the rest of the year the land was normally leased as arable to the highest bidder. In the pasture behind the walls the situation was more complicated. Although the burgesses had traditionally claimed common rights there, the land was actually held by seven landlords, or their leaseholders, to whom rents were paid. In 1570 one of these lessees was Joyce Beanes whose father-in-law had previously acquired a long lease from the Austin Friars, then owners of fourteen acres in the pasture. When in that year the corporation challenged her interest by setting that part of the pasture to three drapers who had agreed to up-grade and extend the conduit, Beanes took them to court in London. She won the case, but later agreed to arrange a sub-lease of the land to the corporation, which in turn sometimes used the pasture as a security for raising money.

The burgesses were fiercely protective of their customary rights, as can be seen from an incident in 1585 when the lawyer Richard Prynce took out a lease from another of the landlords and challenged the town's claim to commons. After sowing part of the land with barley, Prynce sent his farm-hands in May to impound the burgesses' cattle which were still grazing there. A number of boys from town, without telling their parents in case it lost them their rights, attacked the men and drove them off with clods of mud. In this and related disputes the burgesses eventually secured their hold on the pasture behind the walls by buying the landlords out. A potential problem was also raised by a sharp increase in the number of burgesses after 1550 which could have led to the over-stocking of the common pastures. In practice grazing was limited to 30 cows on Kingsland and 30 (later 24) in the pasture behind the walls, with access controlled by a system of burgess 'turns' for each ward. Turns had been devised by at least 1611 and followed the same sequence through the streets as those for the watch.

The burgesses were also anxious to preserve ancient rights of way like the footpath from Kingsland to Meole Brace (now the Cinder Path) mentioned in a survey of the town fields in 1432, and marked on a later sketch map among the Drapers' records. Another such path ran from the Castle Gate to Roushill, passing Garewald's tower on the wall which partly enclosed the river-side meadows there. These included Thornes meadow, one of two closes of that name which probably formed part of the burgage plot extending from Thornes Place, high above in High Pavement, down towards the Severn. There had been disputes with the Thornes family or their tenants over this path in 1464 and 1477 and its course was marked out with stakes; but complaints were still being received in 1544 that John Thornes was obstructing it.

In Tudor Shrewsbury there were three different ways of becoming a burgess or freeman. A few men, usually gentry, were admitted as honorary burgesses. Others obtained the freedom by proving that they were descended from a burgess. But most were admitted by purchase, normally paying a basic entry fine of £2 10s, raised to £5 in 1564. From 1631 aspiring burgesses had also either to have served a seven year apprenticeship or to have been born in Shrewsbury; but these extra conditions were not explicitly stated in the sixteenth century. Admissions by purchase were largely dictated by financial requirements. If the town needed money, the council might decide to hold a 'session' of admissions, which could last up to three days, sometimes longer. Burgesses were admitted on a first come, first served basis - as many as were needed to raise the sums required. The entry fines were quite substantial: in the early sixteenth century £2 10s was equivalent to about a year's income for a building labourer, although small craft masters earned more than this, perhaps £5 to £10. Many craftsmen then had to save up for a few years before they could hope to purchase their freedom.

The most frequent cause for admitting new burgesses was to pay for repairs to the town walls and bridges, or for new buildings like a mill in 1533, school housing in 1552 and the conduit in 1556-7. The actual number of resident burgesses was about 230 in 1530, at least 300 in 1570 and over 400 by the 1580s. They comprised about half of all male householders in 1530, almost 80 per cent in 1560 (after large numbers had been admitted in the 1550s), and perhaps half again by 1585. Those who were not burgesses, known as 'tensors', were allowed to trade on payment of a small fine of 4d, or a bit more if they sold ale.

It is a moot point whether the burgesses always took their duties at assembly seriously. Later, in the 1630s, they were accused of being easily swayed by the opinions of *'popular men'*, and of becoming *'slaves to other men's humours'*. Too often meetings were disrupted by *'4 or 5 brawling fellows'* strategically sited in the Guildhall. Sometimes the Commons bellowed out their approval of motions put to them by the speaker before a debate had even taken place. Certainly some bailiffs seem to have looked on them with contempt. In 1586 Thomas Sherer, sitting on the bailiffs' seat at a 'common hall', told the assembled burgesses that the bailiffs were to be obeyed in all things. When a councillor protested that they were to be obeyed in all things *lawful*, Sherer replied, *'no, we being bailiffs are to be obeyed in all things we command, be it right or wrong, yea, though we be infidels'*. On one occasion, however, the role of the burgesses could not be ignored - the annual civic elections.

Privilege of the people

On Monday 24 June 1594 (Midsummer day) the draper Richard Chirwell was riding with Bailiff Humphrey Hughes to the cloth market at Oswestry when they came across a maypole near the windmill at Cadogan's Cross. Being of puritanical bent they decided to chop it down. Turning back his horse, Chirwell met up with his apprentice Thomas Lacon and told him to fetch a saw or axe. Before Lacon could return, however, the two merchants managed to borrow an axe from the Frankwell constable John Worrall, a prosperous leather worker who in 1576-7 had built a fine timber-framed range on what is now Frankwell roundabout. (The building later became the String of Horses inn; part of the exterior is now preserved at Avoncroft Museum near Bromsgrove.)

Worrall's House

Although Hughes and Chirwell then cut down, the maypole themselves, Lacon was seen later returning to his master's shop

Scrapping with wasters

carrying a saw over his shoulder. For the young shearmen who had set up the tree, this was open provocation. The apprentice Hugh ap Rees in particular spoiled for a fight. He asked Lacon who had told him to fetch the saw. *'My master'*, Lacon replied. *'Then thy master is a woodcock and a whistler'*, ap Rees retorted. They nearly came to blows there and then, but were persuaded to settle it with wasters (wooden staffs) at the fencing school. After scrapping it out for a time, the schoolmaster and others intervened. *'Well'*, ap Rees was heard to say, *'another time will serve'*.

Fencing with sword and dagger

Throughout the summer and autumn he continued to challenge Lacon *'to appoint the field'*. On one occasion at least Lacon rose to the bait, agreeing to fence with sword and dagger at the Weeping Cross near Sutton, but ap Rees failed to turn up. This festering grudge drew in their friends as well; meeting ap Rees in the street one day, Lacon's pal Richard Wright was barged without warning into the side wall.

Ap Rees finally got his fateful revenge on Friday 4 October, the day of the civic elections. It was the practice on that occasion for two common councillors to be selected by lot from a bag. Each councillor, in the presence of the Commons in the Guildhall, then called out the names of twelve burgesses present, and drew lots for another. Together these men comprised the electoral 25. The level of participation was high: at least half of all burgesses alive in 1525, for example, had served one or more times on the 25. In the afternoon they were then shut up in the inner room of the Guildhall without food or drink; there they had to stay until the new officers had been unanimously elected. In 1566 the electors took 26 hours before they could agree; in 1589 they went in at 3 p.m. on Friday and did not get out until 7 p.m. on Saturday. Protracted elections also occurred in 1595, 1600 and 1602 - the choice of the common sergeant in particular was often contentious. While the electors were at their task, the Cornmarket was traditionally given over to the lads, schoolboys and apprentices of the town. It was a time for searching out enemies and settling old scores. In 1594 ap Rees and his friend William Morris, son of another shearman, talked prospects over in the afternoon at the door to the Stillyard, a complex of buildings, adjacent to the Sextry tavern, and the Mercers' Hall. *'Wilt thou come abroad soon at night?'* asked Morris. *'I cannot tell'*, said ap Rees, *'but if I can leave work I will'*. *'Then'*, Morris replied, *'I will come look for thee, for I mean to beat two or three this night'*. Between 8 and 9 o'clock the electors were still deliberating. Among their number that year was Richard Chirwell himself; Lacon was waiting outside in the dark with his mates, near his master's shop in the Cornmarket. Morris and ap Rees approached him with their staffs.

Petty insults soon led to violence, and Lacon was smashed upon the skull. His assailants ran off into the dark, chased by witnesses. Lacon was carried indoors, pale and clammy: shortly after he was dead.

Lacon's murder, like the case of the Shearmen's tree, created a sensation in Shrewsbury. It also confirmed the worst fears of those puritans who despised the tradition of Election night disorder. Already in 1583 an attempt had been made to ban the custom, evidently without success. For more sober members of the civic élite, the whole form of the election and its attendant customs had begun to seem too populist and vulgar. Their criticisms came to a head in 1637. It was said that when the two councillors made their nominations for the 25, the assembly was rent with *'such incivility and rudeness that few of the better sort will be there, so that the 25 that choose the bailiffs are most of them very mean persons'*. The 25 were supposed to be impartial, but people slipped bits of paper into their pockets suggesting names to vote for. Closeted together, they spent most of their time smoking tobacco and playing cards. If they couldn't agree, they would threaten to *'starve one another and eat the brawn off their arms before they will yield'*. Meanwhile the town clerk -

claiming that the custom was a *'privilege of the people'* - allowed all the *'rascality'* of the town to lark about in the Cornmarket, singing obscene songs until the election was over. But it was a privilege that had had its time. In 1638 a new charter swept away the old system which had lasted 200 years. The two bailiffs were replaced by one mayor, selected by rota from the aldermen. All the other civic officers were now chosen by an enlarged town council. Although public meetings were sometimes held in later decades, the institutional role of the Commons was effectively abolished: except for parliamentary elections, they never met in common hall again.

What of Lacon's killers? After capture they tried desperately to pin the blame on each other. But on 29 October they were indicted by the Grand Jury and sent for trial. They were found guilty of murder and sentenced to die. Next day in the afternoon they were taken to Old Heath and hanged;

'they died with patience repenting their former lives to the example of all youths and people present, at whose execution were a great multitude'.

Chapter 3 - Population, Trade and Markets

A growing population

The central fact in Shrewsbury's history during the Tudor period was the growth of the town's population which more than doubled in the century after 1550. Including the Abbey Foregate suburb, the number of inhabitants had fluctuated between about 3,000 and 3,300 in the first half of the sixteenth century. By 1587 the population had grown to about 5,500, as high if not higher than the previous peak reached before the Black Death in 1348-9; it rose further to slightly more than 7,000 by 1640. The totals seem tiny now: fewer people lived in Shrewsbury in 1550 than do today in a commuter village like Bayston Hill. Even so, for contemporaries the consequences of population growth were far-reaching. Examples have already been noted, including the way increasing numbers of burgesses threatened the ecology of the commons, and how a rise in the number of aspiring councillors promoted municipal corruption. In the rural liberties too there were similar problems. By 1589, for example, the inhabitants of Acton Reynald were complaining of the number of squatting cottages being erected at Grinshill and of the *'great number of vagrant wandering people'* resorting there. Novel problems and anxieties of this kind became a typical experience of the time.

From Great Court lists of adult male householders (see chapter 5), we can get a good idea of the way in which the growth of the population was distributed through the town. Together with the suburbs, the central streets were at first able to absorb nearly all the new householders. After 1575, however, continued growth also required the development of outlying streets which, as the 'Burghley' map of about 1575 shows, still had extensive plots and gardens on which to build - Murivance (Swan Hill), St. John's Hill and Claremont Hill (see back cover). In Murivance, there were only seven or eight male householders in 1563 and 1576, but 32 in 1613 and 40 in 1629, including many clothworkers. This increase shows up well on surviving maps. On the Burghley map Murivance barely appears, its course still mostly covered by gardens. On Speed's map of 1610 (overleaf), however, the street is clearly marked, with housing extending down much of its length. After 1613 the rate of increase within the walls slowed down considerably, although suburban growth was still quite dynamic. Of the suburbs Castle Foregate showed the biggest change: in 1563 it had just thirteen male householders compared with 63 in 1634. In fact, of all the streets in Shrewsbury only Murivance grew faster in the century after 1563. Taken as a whole, the number of male householders in the town (excluding the Abbey Foregate) rose from 437 in the spring of 1563 to 1,072 in 1634. Including the Abbey Foregate, numbers rose from about 800 in 1587 to 1,266 in 1634.

One consequence of the growth of population was a great increase in marketing and inland trade. Toll receipts at the town and Abbey Foregate fairs almost trebled between 1560 and 1640, and by 1600 residents of Coleham and Abbey Foregate were complaining that the road approaching the Stone Bridge was being worn away by the numbers of country people travelling to Shrewsbury's markets. Over a thousand yards of re-paving was needed. There was also a great rise in litigation involving credit - either informal sales credit or sealed acknowledgements of sums to be paid, known as bonds.

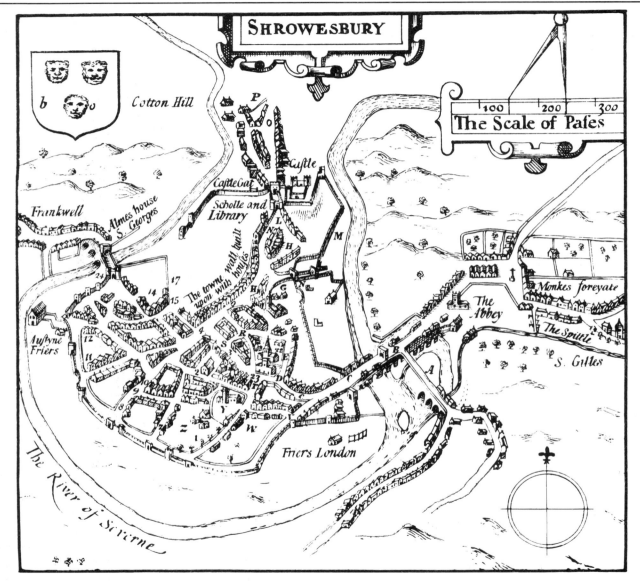

SHROWESBURY

b   o

Cotton Hill

The Scale of Pafes
100   200   300

P

O

Caftle

CaftleGat

Scholle and
Library

Frankwell

Almes house
S. Georges

L
N
H
M

24

14   17
15   H   G
N

The towne wall built
won with houfes

Austyne
Friers

12   R

11

Monkes foreyate

The Abbey

The Spittle

S. Gilles

2   13
10   C
9   Y   C
8   B

Z   W   A

1

Friers London

The River of Severne

In the fifty years after 1560 lawsuits of this kind in the town court more than doubled. In the central law courts at Westminster the number of cases concerning disputed bonds sealed in Shrewsbury rose more than ten-fold in the same period. Many of these cases involved prospering gentry and yeomen farmers from Shropshire, Montgomeryshire and north Wales who had begun to visit Shrewsbury in large numbers to borrow money.

Market expansion was also reflected by the rise of the Welsh cloth trade which in Shrewsbury attained its greatest prosperity in the century after 1540. It is now known that the origins of this manufacture in areas such as the Tanat and Ceiriog valleys can be traced back to the fourteenth century. But its development in north Wales and the northern Marches was especially marked after 1450 and important markets grew up at Oswestry and Welshpool, changing the pattern of regional trade. Shrewsbury's own markets were at first badly affected by this competition, and there was a severe drop in toll income. Measures were taken in 1470 and 1500 to correct the situation, and Salopians were asked to *'courteously entreat all strangers that resort to the said town and righteously demean* [flatter] *them in buying and selling'*. In fact, despite these problems, Shrewsbury began to benefit in other ways. Its merchants increasingly took control of the cloth trade, buying from the farmer-weavers in the border markets and bringing the cloth to Shrewsbury for finishing. The number of master shearmen (clothworkers) rose from less than a dozen in 1398 to 70 in 1525 and 81 in 1553. Without their presence the town's economy would have been in serious trouble before 1550. Looking back in April 1586, the residents of Knockyn Street (Hill's Lane) could recall a time when rents for houses, chambers and shops had all risen because of the number of shearmen setting up in town. Once the population began to grow as a whole, their numbers grew even further to 118 masters in 1569 and about 200 in 1587.

The impact of plague

Plague swelling in groin (from a 15th century painting)

In 1631 the feltmaker Edmund Eley was asked by the bailiffs to check the bodies of John Griffithes' daughter and the glover John Balle who had both died within a few days of falling ill. As the authorities feared, Eley reported back *'that they had the marks upon them'*. These were the spots beneath the skin, changing colour between orange and black, blue and purple, which were typical symptoms of bubonic plague. Others include swellings of the lymph glands in the groin, armpit or neck. In January 1519, for example, Matilda Heynes swore on oath before the bailiffs that she had seen John Genno sick with plague in his house, with tell-tale signs behind his left ear. The disease itself is caused by a bacillus carried to humans from infected fleas deserting dead or dying rodents, the Black Rat especially in this period. The toxins released by the bacillus act extremely fast, and most victims, like Balle and Griffithes' daughter, died within days of infection. Since plague depends on fleas it thrives in warm conditions when the fleas can breed rapidly, and for this reason is usually associated with the summer and autumn months. All the worst Shrewsbury epidemics - in 1526, 1536, 1576, 1604, 1631 and 1650 - happened at that season, although plague can persist in the winter months if sufficient fleas survive in the warmth of rodent nests. Genno's plight was a good example. Plague had broken out in St. Alkmund's parish in the summer of 1518 when the meat stalls were moved from Fish Street to the High Street as a precaution, and Genno's infection next January was a left-over from the summer outbreak.

Plague may have helped to restrict population increase in the first half of the sixteenth century, but once the upward trend became really marked after 1560, epidemics had surprisingly little effect. The worst outbreak in 1604 killed about ten per cent of the population, although this was quite a modest mortality rate compared to some towns. But, as with the other epidemics after 1560, including a serious typhus outbreak in 1587, these losses were quickly made good, which incidentally shows the importance of immigration in contributing to Shrewsbury's growth. For the majority of townsfolk it was the psychological impact of plague, and the way it restricted their daily lives, that affected them most.

Plague tended to spread across the country in epidemic waves, sometimes lasting for several years at a time, and most of the Shrewsbury outbreaks can be linked to the presence of the disease elsewhere. One such wave occurred in 1563-5, but in this case

Shrewsbury was lucky. The precautions taken in 1563 were typical. Proclamations were stuck up on the three gates of the town prohibiting any traveller from London or any other infected community from coming within four miles of the town and its liberties. Salopians themselves were forbidden to take in lodgers from infected places, or to receive merchant wares, clothes and other *'household stuffs'* which might have come from there. Two craftsmen who disobeyed these instructions were imprisoned and their shops closed. Similar measures were taken in 1593. Plague was raging in London and other towns; a strict watch and ward was imposed to turn away infected persons, and although the disease was reported in Bishop's Castle and Wem and as close as three miles away, the town was spared.

The triumph of death, 17th century

Shrewsbury was less fortunate in 1576. The epidemic was particularly virulent in the parishes of St. Alkmund and St. Chad, both of which lost their curates to the disease. A list was drawn up of some thirty infected houses, most of them lying in these parishes. To judge from the burial register, the mortality rate in St. Alkmund's almost doubled while the plague ran its course. The council ordered all pigs and dogs to be removed and cats killed; the streets to be cleaned every Wednesday and Saturday, and back lanes swept once a week; mixens (dunghills) and water ditches to be cleaned and emptied; and fires lit on alternate nights in the streets to prevent the spread of infection. Such measures reflected the belief that plague stemmed from a miasma which could be carried not only in polluted air but also contagiously by domestic animals and in fabrics and clothes. This led naturally to the idea that victims should be quarantined, a view officially supported by the government in 1578 which also required magistrates to raise local taxes for the relief of the sick. All these practices were adopted in Shrewsbury, including the provision of a pesthouse for the sick. In 1604 the ruined chapel at Cadogan's Cross was repaired for the purpose, although the facility was later sited on Kingsland. The shoemaker John Meighen was pardoned various fines in 1631 after administering medicines at the pesthouse under the guidance of the surgeon William Boraston who also wrote a tract about the plague.

Plague epidemics brought normal life almost to a standstill. In 1536 the civic elections were suspended and the fairs were poorly attended, while in 1576, 1604 and 1631 toll receipts at the fairs shrank to nothing and lawsuits at the Small Court virtually disappeared. One serious problem was that farmers were discouraged from bringing corn to market. In 1576 both the lawyer Richard Prynce of Abbey Foregate and Sir Andrew Corbet (who built Moreton Corbet castle) offered their help to provision the town. Prynce, who lost a relative in the outbreak, compared the bailiffs to Moses and Aaron charged by God to lead the Israelites from the wilderness. Only careful diligence would calm the rage of the poor, desperate for bread. As he put it, *'let not the sheep perish by default of the shepherd'*. The authorities were not always inclined to follow this advice. During the 1536 plague most of the aldermen absented themselves from council meetings. Not surprisingly there was considerable hostility among the less fortunate who found themselves subject to quarantine orders. In 1604 the tailor Thomas Browne refused to be cooped up in an infected house, shouting at the bailiffs that he *'would walk and go abroad in despite of any whomsoever would say to the contrary'*. In 1631 the whole of Frankwell, centre of the epidemic, was quarantined, provoking a riot when some of the residents attempted unsuccessfully to smash their way across the Welsh Bridge. At the same time fear of death boosted church

attendance. At Michaelmas 1576 at the height of the epidemic, *'a great number of every parish in the town'* came to St. Mary's to receive communion; and shortly after the 1631 plague, the minister Thomas Lloyd claimed that at the risk of infection he had kept morning prayer throughout the epidemic at St. Alkmund's church, *'where the people of the said town do daily resort in a greater number than formerly they did'*. By contrast, the masters and pupils of the grammar school were able to escape to a house at Grinshill, built especially to house them during epidemics in town. Completed in 1617, it was used by the school in both 1631 and 1650 and still survives.

The great rebuilding

The growth of population and the profits to be made from the boom in trade and litigation meant that Shrewsbury experienced a great rebuilding after 1560. The evidence for this is most obvious in the houses built for the town's prosperous merchants and lawyers - such as Ireland's Mansion, Owen's Mansion, Jones's Mansion in Dogpole, Proude's Mansion, Perche's Mansion, Rowley's House and Mansion, and Prynce's Place

Arms on Perche's Mansion

Jones's Mansion, Under the Wyle

('Whitehall') in the Abbey Foregate. To these one might add the Drapers' Hall, built between 1576 and 1582, and a new wing to Rigg's Hall, built for the headmaster of the grammar school in Rotten Lane and finished in 1589. In the case of Perche's Mansion we know that the property was purchased by the wool merchant John Perche in January 1581 for £43 10s from John Bromhall of Northwood Hall; the conveyance describes the site exactly as it is today, stretching from High Pavement (Castle Street) to St. Mary's churchyard. Perche added the date, his initials and arms to a tie-beam, although this may record the purchase rather than the fact that he built the house himself. These are buildings that survive, but there were others that have not. Apart from Sherer's Mansion (c. 1620), Worrall's House (1576-7) and Thornes Hall (c. 1625) already mentioned,

Weale's window

they included Lloyd's Mansion (1570) at the corner of the Cornmarket and Kiln Lane; Gibbons's Mansion lying behind houses on Wyle Cop which was built for the attorney Nicholas Gibbons who practised in the central law courts and was elected bailiff in 1588 and 1596; Jones's Mansion, which stood on the right as one came over the Stone Bridge (although the beautiful oriel window overlooking an inner courtyard dated to 1575 was erected by the previous occupant, the dyehouse owner William Weale); Merivale House on the other side of the bridge (1601); and the front range of Bellstone Hall (c. 1582) in Romaldesham, built by Edward Owen of the Drapers' company who served as bailiff on four occasions between 1582 and 1603. In addition, about 1610 Sir Humphrey Lee of Langley and Lea Hall, Preston Gubbals, built the Stone House, a tall town residence erected against the town wall almost opposite the east end of St. Mary's. Some of these houses, such as Owen's and Lloyd's mansions, were probably intended for one family, with a dwelling above a shop. But others were built as investments, of which Ireland's Mansion in High Street is an outstanding example. There were two branches of this merchant family at this date, and it is not completely certain which one was responsible for erecting this building, but clues suggest it was built about the 1560s for the Irelands of Lythwood Hall and Shrewsbury.

Bellstone Hall

Ireland's Mansion

Shut driven through Bennett's Hall

While part was retained for the family's use (for example, when the children came from Lythwood to attend school), the other chambers, ground-floor shops and cellars were rented out. Family wills indicate that the Irelands were not themselves the landlords of the site which belonged to the Vernons. They in turn had inherited properties in town belonging to the Ludlows of Stokesay Castle who had been the greatest of all the wool merchants of medieval Shrewsbury.

Development of this kind comprised one way of housing the growing population and satisfying demand for additional shops. Alternatively one could build over existing backyards and gardens or subdivide older properties. An example was the fate of the medieval stone building known as Bennett's Hall (the remains of which are incorporated in Evans, 2 Pride Hill): it was partially demolished at this time and the site colonized by timber-framed cottages served by an alley or 'shut', known much later as Leopard shut. Development brought its own problems. In September 1585, for instance, an inquest of jurymen heard that by erecting a new house in Shoplatch the landlord Geoffrey Jones had blocked a water course which had run through the backyards of several tenements in the street.

Much of the land in Shrewsbury consisted of burgage plots stretching back from the street. Many of these plots were part of the town estate, for which rents, often nominal, were paid. As people erected new shops and built up on backyards and 'void grounds', they had in many cases to pay additional rents to the corporation. In September 1579, for example, Richard Reignolds was leased a piece of waste ground in Carnarvon Lane to build upon, provided he left part of his freehold elsewhere in the lane to help widen it. These 'new takings' added about fifteen per cent to the value of corporation rents between 1550 and 1580, and included marginal properties like the towers on the town walls which had previously been unoccupied. All the same the council had to order surveys in 1563, 1568 and 1570 to check the scale of illegal encroachments.

In many streets the density of inhabitants rose substantially. Poorer families in particular suffered from living in squalid

Arms of Owen of Bellstone Hall and Woodhouse

tenements or one-roomed cottages, often run up in courts and alleys off the street, as in the area known later as the 'rookery' behind the present Post Office in St. Mary's Street. Later surveys of the poor hint at the kind of conditions that existed. In the mid seventeenth century, for example, the landlord Edward Owen, Esq., of Bellstone Hall and Woodhouse, owned a tenement in Shoplatch in which, in addition to the tenant Edward Farmer, there lived one sub-tenant, the shearman Thomas Morris with his wife and three children in lodgings with no chimney for a fire; and the beggar Thomas ap Richard with his two year old son.

In the suburbs cramped conditions were also common, and an incident in Frankwell about 1632 shows the kind of tensions that could arise in these confined spaces. Robert Davis lived in a shut which led from the street to a court around which several other tenants lived. To enter the court the tenants had to open a door which had fallen off its hinges two years before. For the time being Davis had propped it up against his wall. But since the wall now needed repairs, Davis had moved the door aside, throwing his neighbour, Widow Mary Morris, into a towering rage. She abused him as a rogue, a rascal and a thief, and threw a chamber pot of urine and two kettlefuls of water over him as he was walking down the shut. He did not retaliate but went out to find the constable. While he was away Morris and her two daughters also beat up his son George. That at least was his story as recited in his petition to the bailiffs. The widow's account, written for her from the Welsh Gate prison, was different. She claimed that she was coming back late on a Saturday evening from working in the fields when she found the door had been moved from its storage place. As she tried to put it back, George Davis ran out swearing, calling her a *'base'* and a *'rotten whore'*, and had thrashed her and her little, lame boy with a staff. The bailiffs were not inclined to believe this version, however. Morris was kept in prison and later fined for an affray, the fine payable in instalments.

Markets and fairs

After the poet and adventurer Thomas Churchyard, who was born in Shrewsbury, had revisited the town in 1587, he wrote, *'I walked the streets and marked what came to view. Found old things dead, as world were made anew'*.

Riding to market

Another sign of these changes was the appearance of new market facilities. In 1566-7 two timber-framed bays with a loft above were erected in the Cornmarket for sheltering corn, and another pair were added by two carpenters, partly at their own expense, in return for their burgess-ship. Three more bays were built in 1569-70 paid for by Alderman Humphrey Onslow, whose nephew Richard, Speaker of the House of Commons, died on a visit to Shrewsbury in 1571. All these bays were taken down in March 1596 and replaced by the present Market Hall. The first stone was laid on 15 June and the whole building was virtually finished by the time the bailiffs left office at Michaelmas. The presiding contractor was almost certainly Walter Hancock, a successful mason from Much Wenlock who had worked for the Newport and Owen families at High Ercall and Condover Hall.

The corn market was held every Wednesday and Saturday. We can get an idea of the farmers who supplied the market from the schedules drawn up in November and December 1550 for provisioning the town at a time of grain shortages and high prices. The schedules are not complete, but they show that 113 farmers from the town's rural liberties were included in the scheme, from Clive in the north to Sutton in the south; while 144 other farmers came from a quadrant south of the Severn, stretching to Much Wenlock, beneath Wenlock Edge to Hope Bowdler, and north again from Stretton to Condover. In addition, twelve farmers came from Millichope and Easthope on Wenlock Edge itself, and six from Stanton Long and Holdgate in Corve Dale.

One of the places mentioned in the schedules was Cardington. In September 1529 two farmers from that hamlet contracted to supply Charlton castle at Wrockwardine, belonging to Edward Grey, the lord of Powys, with 36 bushels of *'good and able rye, of dry corn, clean corn and well winnowed'* before the first week of Lent 1530. Grey's servant obviously thought the deal important enough to have it registered in the Shrewsbury court book. The bushel measure to be used was that kept by the Shrewsbury baker John Wartoner who lived on the Wyle (the slope of what we now know as Wyle Cop). Other craftsmen provided similar facilities. In 1563 a measure was kept at the house of the shearman John Meredythe, *'being a place accustomed to measure all kind of grain'*. Their bushels no doubt were reckoned to be 'Shrewsbury measure', that is of 40 quarts, compared to the 32 quarts of the standard Winchester bushel used throughout the south-east.

On a more regional level, court records show that Shrewsbury had market links throughout the upper Severn valley and beyond to Machynlleth. In 151 Rees ap Deio Gough of Machynlleth sued a carrier from Chester for detaining three pieces of armour worth £6 in all, a substantial sum. The bargain for delivery must have been made in Shrewsbury, otherwise the case could not have been brought there. As one would expect, Shrewsbury also had trading links down the river Severn, and through the West Midlands to London. Coventry in particular, with its own drapery for Welsh cloths, was an important market for Shrewsbury merchants. Before the Reformation they attended banquets of the Coventry Corpus Christi guild, and also became members of the city's prestigious Holy Trinity guild - a religious and mutual benefit society for prominent townspeople and gentry. When the Shrewsbury mercer William Luter made his will in 1527 he asked to be buried in St. Michael's Church, Coventry; and the will of another Shrewsbury merchant John Lynde, who died in 1540, shows that his brother Oliver worked in that city. Not all the links were one way. In 1535 Julian Nethermill of Coventry, one of the richest merchants in England, sued the glover Richard Hatton in the town court for a large debt of £15, which shows he must have done business in Shrewsbury.

Going at a steady pace on horseback, men with business in London could reach the capital in four days. In 1526, for example, three important citizens travelled to London about a river dispute with Worcester. Leaving Shrewsbury early on Friday 27 April they lodged at Shifnal for the night. On the second day they stopped at Wolverhampton to feed their horses, and later spent 1s 4d for a snack at Birmingham. Saturday night was spent at Coventry, where 4d was also given to a friar to sing mass. On Sunday the route took them down Watling Street, stopping at Daventry to feed their horses and at Towcester for a drink. Sunday night was spent at Stony Stratford, and London was reached on Monday after stops at Dunstable for dinner and St. Albans for another snack. On a previous visit the preceding November, a dinner for two at London had cost between 7d and 1s, and supper between 8d and 1s 1d. Three pairs of shoes were

Apple Market, 1600

also bought for 2s, their shorts were washed for 3d, and 2d was also spent for a shave on the Saturday night they arrived and on the following Tuesday - presumably a penny a man. For comparison, Shrewsbury carpenters at this date were paid 5d a day, and a pound of candles cost 1 1/2d.

Several other markets also existed in Shrewsbury. The livestock market was held in Frankwell on Saturdays, although complaints were made in 1566 and 1570 that the bailiffs were allowing beasts to be sold at the High Cross instead. Hides and skins could be purchased on Pride Hill until 1655 when the market was kept on Wednesdays in a cellar at the bottom of St. John's Hill. The apple market for fruit and vegetables was held at the High Street end of the Cornmarket; while butter (which was sold by the 'dish'), cheese, geese, pigs and poultry were sold at the High Cross, as orders of 1583-4 instructed.

Poultry for the High Cross

In May 1594 the butter market was covered with *'timber work for country folks and others to sit and stand dry from rain'*. An earlier order in 1540 indicates that bread could also be

bought there. With the growth of markets after 1560, important developments took place in the scale of dairy farming in the north Shropshire plain, which was an extension of the Cheshire cheese country, and London dealers began to appear at the market scouring for supplies. In 1595 the London ironmonger Richard Olliver was prevented from carting 72 great cheeses, valued at £18, down to London. They had been bought in Shrewsbury which was then suffering from a shortage of provisions.

Meat could be bought at the fleshboards in Fish Street (which then included Butcher Row), but not on a Friday which was a fish day. The fish market was also kept there until 1648 when it was moved to St. John's Hill. It was said to be intolerable that both markets were kept in the same place. Access to St. Alkmund's church was often blocked, and butchers were accused of buying up the fish themselves for resale, to the detriment of the poor. A case in point involved the butcher Thomas Hamonde who in March 1574 bought a barrel of 80 salted herrings in Fish Street for 23s 9d. Not everyone agreed to the market's relocation. Among those who wanted to retain the old site was Henry Carter from Bangor. Like other travelling fishmongers, he had got used to lodging at inns close by. His presence shows that fish was brought in from north Wales, but the North Sea would also have supplied the town. In 1513 the draper Hugh Blanea purchased saltfish from John Blake of Littleover (near Derby), presumably a middleman bringing fish from the east coast, although herrings are also known to have been imported from Chester and Bristol.

Shrewsbury did not manage to capture the main cloth market from Oswestry until the 1620s. By 1629 market day was held on a Wednesday at the Market Hall, but this was later moved to Friday, and then back to Thursday after complaints in 1649 from ministers at Dolgellau and elsewhere that parishioners visiting Shrewsbury had insufficient time to return for the Sabbath. Cloths themselves could only be bought between the hours of noon and 5 p.m. in summer, and from noon to 4 p.m.

Fishmongers

in winter. This was a very typical measure aimed at securing fair access for all to the market. In 1532, for example, fish hawkers were ordered not to buy produce displayed at the market before 11 a.m. Similarly, the Tanners prohibited any master from buying hides and skins before 8 a.m., and purchases could only be made in open market and not at the slaughterhouses (1606). Townsfolk were traditionally opposed to 'forestalling' - the purchase of wares and produce before they could get to open market. In 1549 there were complaints that Welsh women bringing butter, cheese and eggs to market were being intercepted at the gates. It was an ancient problem, but one that became increasingly common as the complexity and scale of markets increased. By 1640 the Tanners' company were complaining of the amount of private dealing taking place at inns, while they themselves were accused in 1641 by the shoemakers of selling *'their leather in private, as in their own houses and storehouses'*.

In addition to these markets, four fairs were also held. The two town fairs began on the Wednesday before Whitsun and on St. Matthew's day (21 September), while the Abbey Foregate by 1562 held fairs beginning on 22 June and 1 August. Two more fairs were also added in 1638. During the town fairs, in the early sixteenth century at least, the toll booths at the gates were decorated with greenery, herbs and flowers; while licences to beg in the form of canvas tokens, painted with leopard heads, were also handed out to the poor. Although other products were sold, including wool, timber, fruit and cheese, the fairs were best known for livestock sales, especially cattle and horses. Shrewsbury was a centre for drove routes from Montgomeryshire and north Wales, and was an important outlet for Welsh cattle. At the Michaelmas fair in 1588, for example, Thomas Heylin of Shropshire bought 95 oxen and cows from David ap Howell of Merionethshire. Sales had to be registered, and parties paid 4d toll for each transaction, although sellers at weekly markets had been toll free since 1500. Tokens were also handed out to purchasers of livestock, apparently as proof that they had paid toll. Gradually the fairs tended to specialize and attract different kinds of dealers. The Whitsun fair, for instance, was noted for dairy animals and was popular with dealers from Lancashire and Cheshire, while separate fairs developed for old, fat or fresh draught oxen. Over the whole year, however, more cattle were sold at the weekly markets, which involved a more local traffic, than at the fairs. In 1598 421 cattle were sold at the fairs and 611 at the markets - although that particular year was a poor one for trade.

Shrewsbury fairs were also well known for horse sales. In fact both market sites in Frankwell and Abbey Foregate were known as the 'horsefair'. In 1578, however, following a prolonged drought, many dealers at the Michaelmas fair in 1578 took their horses out on to the dried-up bed of the river Severn and struck their bargains there instead. Many of the animals sold were sturdy ponies or 'merlins' brought in from the great common pastures of Montgomeryshire. A large slice of the trade comprised the sale of these ponies to colliers, metal workers, carriers and other tradesmen, especially to the area of north Worcestershire and south Staffordshire where mines and manufactures were springing up. The trade illustrates again the way in which Shrewsbury acted as a market interchange between England and the uplands of Wales.

Chapter 4 - **Households and Companies**

Households

At the heart of Salopian society lay the domestic household. In the 1520s about 320 of these households were headed by masters in one of the craft fellowships (excluding the Abbey Foregate), and another 120 by males outside the craft system, including not only labourers, but also doctors, lawyers and others working in unusual occupations, like the drover Thomas Pyper who lived in Mardol. In addition there were about 110 households headed by widows and single women (of whom twenty or so were 'sisters' in one of the craft fellowships), and about twenty households kept by journeymen. Such men did not usually keep their own households unless they were married; otherwise they put up in lodgings. In 1613 21 single journeymen were working in Corvisors Row (Pride Hill), of whom seventeen lodged with other households (six with a parent), and four were boarding with the masters for whom they worked.

The proportion of households made up of these different groups probably changed little in the century after 1520. To judge from evidence from other towns, about forty per cent of households at any one time would have kept servants, including domestics. The actual number in each household varied according to the wealth of the master or mistress, and the nature of the trade in which they worked. We can get some indication of the variations that existed from a muster list in 1573 of mostly male householders and their male servants aged sixteen years or more. Altogether almost forty per cent of these households kept male servants, although in most of the suburbs the percentage was much less - only twenty-six per cent in Castle Foregate,

for instance, and fifteen per cent in Coleham. That was due to the large number of poor labourers living in those areas who could not afford to employ servants.

It is interesting to note which craftsmen had the largest number of male servants. Three members of the Corvisors' (Shoemakers') craft had five servants each, as did the tanner George Higgons who served as bailiff on five occasions between 1563 and 1587. These men were obviously engaged in large-scale leather production requiring a large domestic workforce. Then came the carpenter Roger Smyth with six male servants. Originally from Llandysilio in Montgomeryshire, Smyth was responsible for framing the Drapers' Hall in 1576. He was in effect a building contractor. Among his servants was Randle Sandford, whose father John Sandford had been responsible for framing Pitchford Hall about 1550. But the craftsman with the largest number of male servants - nine - was the dyer Richard Gardiner who lived in Frankwell. His dye works must have been on a considerable scale for him to have kept such a large household. In December 1584 one of his servants accidentally fell into one of the vats and was scalded to death. Gardiner was obviously something of an entrepreneur. He was chiefly responsible for bringing the conduit in lead pipes to the top of Corvisors Row in 1573, from where branches ran to Wyle Cop, the High Street wall of the Sextry tavern, the apple market by the Guildhall, and Mardol Head. In 1579 he also enclosed the springs by the Conduit Head (at Broadwell near Crowmeole), using a plan drawn up in the Exchequer. The waters were then directed to the Head itself, a timber-framed building which still survives. In addition Gardiner unearthed a coal seam in March

Conduit Head in the 19th century

1573 near Emstrey, part of the Shrewsbury-Hanwood coalfield, and he was also a keen horticulturalist (see chapter 7).

Men like Gardiner represented the pinnacle of success in the domestic economy, reached after years of schooling, service and hard work as a craft master. This was the ideal progression, but many others were left far behind. By the 1570s the corporation had begun to develop a system of poor relief, and records show that in normal years about eight per cent of the population were maintained by the ratepayers. The majority of recipients were women, often from Wales, scraping a living from carding wool, spinning, taking in washing or begging. These were the 'booked' poor. But in crisis years when the town was hit by dearth or epidemic disease, emergency doles were also paid out. At such times the number of people on relief could double, including many poorer craftsmen, unable to keep their businesses afloat.

Schooling

The Old School buildings in Castle Gates are among the most familiar in Shrewsbury. The original north part was erected from 1594 to 1612, and a cross wing was added from 1627 to 1630. This wing incorporates the entrance with the figures of two scholars on either side, each standing on part of an inscription in Greek from Isocrates: *'If you are a lover of learning, you will become very learned'*. The school itself had been founded earlier - in 1552 - although the idea for a foundation had been around for several years. In 1530 the merchant David Ireland (father of Robert Ireland senior) had left in his will money to purchase lands for a chantry *'or else a free school'*. Nor was it the first school of its type in Shrewsbury - a grammar school is mentioned in a court case in 1439. But it was the sixteenth century institution that began to flourish in an unprecedented way, especially after the keen protestant Thomas Ashton became headmaster in 1561. It was his Ordinances, finally adopted in 1578 seven years after his resignation, which regulated the school for more than two centuries.

By the 1580s the school was perhaps the largest in England, with about three to four hundred scholars, and its importance is demonstrated by the architectural merit of the north wing, built of Grinshill stone, which must have been an imposing building on its site. From the admission registers we can tell that about two thirds of the boys at this date came from outside Shrewsbury. The school was particularly popular with gentry families from Shropshire and north Wales, whose fathers, as we have noted, were increasingly visiting town on business and to borrow money. When holidays ended and the boarders returned to Shrewsbury, the population of the town must have grown by almost five per cent. It is not surprising then that by 1586 the streeters of Knockyn Street (Hill's Lane) were complaining that chambers were being let to scholars at *'an exceeding great rent as thereby it is that no poor man can have any house at a reasonable rent'* - and this despite the fact that scholars were being lodged two, three or even four to a room.

The Old School

The age of admission varied, but the average was about ten, and boys could expect to stay at school for a little over five years, although life for some of the boarders at least was obviously a misery. In May 1590 the Welsh lad Rees ap John, aged about twelve and an idle boy who *'hated the school'*, hanged himself in his own room. Admission fees were graduated, ranging from 10s for the son of a lord, to 8d for sons of Salopians or 4d if you were the son of a burgess. The school itself was divided into three parts or 'schools', each supervised by a master.

By the 1580s there was also a separate petty or 'accidence' school for young beginners, where reading, writing and simple arithmetic were taught. This petty school was not the only one in Shrewsbury: in 1624, for example, one of the prisoners in the Welsh Gate kept a school there for *'many good men's children'*. To enter the main school it was necessary to have acquired basic skills because new boys had to be able to write their names, read English and know some elementary grammar.

Once admitted, scholars were taught the classics (mainly Latin authors), and encouraged to turn a poetic phrase. When John Baker the second master died in 1607, the scholars pinned

A petty school

verses on to the black cloth covering the hearse. Ashton's own theatrical interests were also influential. The top form had to perform an act from a comedy once a week, and the boys themselves probably participated in the Whitsun plays. On several occasions the school also laid on displays or pageants for the visiting Council in the Marches, as in May 1581 when the Lord President Sir Henry Sidney, who was leaving Shrewsbury by barge, was greeted by several scholars on an island downstream of the Castle. Dressed as green nymphs with willow branches tied to their heads, they recited verses across the water: *'And will your honour needs depart, and must it needs be so.*

Would God we could like fishes swim, that we might with thee go'. The Lord President, whose own son Philip had been admitted to the school in 1564, was brought close to tears.

Many Salopians probably found this a lot of high-brow rubbish. At least one craftsman is known to have expressed open hostility towards snooty gentry boarders. In October 1641 the cook William Wodden heard that his son (who was not at the school) had been insulted by the scholar Robert Eyton, son of Sir Robert Eyton J.P. of Dudleston near Ellesmere. He stormed out into the street near the school, grabbed hold of Eyton and gave him a good beating with a stick, shouting out that Eyton's father was a pimp and *'that his son was as good a man's son as the said Robert Eyton'*, adding that unlike Eyton's father, he had never been a butter seller in Oswestry.

In fact, as far as townsfolk were concerned, the educational opportunities provided by the school were not as important as one might think. In the 1570s, for instance, probably less than one tenth of households would have had a boy at the school at any one time. The cost of paying for instruction at a 'petty', and buying stationery and books, as well as the loss of a son's labour, would have discouraged many artisans from sending their boys to school.

On the other hand, there is good evidence that ordinary townsfolk did feel that they had a stake in the school, even though only a minority actually sent their boys there. This is illustrated by a famous incident in 1608. After the second master John Baker had died in 1607, the headmaster John Meighen and the bailiffs quarrelled over the appointment of his successor. Meighen wanted to promote Ralph Gittins the third master, but the bailiffs, for various reasons, opposed him. On Wednesday 31 August 1608 the bailiffs came to the school formally to install Simon Moston who had been recommended by St. John's College, Cambridge, whose fellows had a say in the choice of new masters. But the building had already been occupied that morning by two men and about sixty women, including three spinsters, two widows, and the wives of mercers, tailors, weavers, butchers, shoemakers, tanners, glovers, carpenters, coopers and other tradesmen. Jamming the school benches up against the door, they barricaded themselves in until Saturday, refusing to allow the authorities to enter, and claiming that only the son of a burgess, such as Gittins, could serve as second master. When the bailiffs tried to read out the Statute on Rebellion, the women hollered and stamped on the floorboards, preventing anyone from hearing what was said. From time to time the ringleaders also passed around a *'great hammer'* which had been used to gain entry to the school.

Eventually the women came out after receiving an assurance that Moston would not be made master, although 29 of them were still indicted later for riot at the town sessions, the court which dealt with criminal offences. The trial jury sat on 20 September, but was unable to come to a clear verdict. Four days later the bailiffs tried again. This time about forty people, including Gittins himself, shut them out. When the bailiffs tried to come up the stairs, Gittins hurled down *'a great piece of timber'*, and turning to the window, shouted out to the crowd outside, *'Come in burgesses, come in, for here I do stand on your right'*. The fourth master Ralph Jones then opened the door, and dozens poured in, including the headmaster's wife, bawling *'down with the bailiffs'*. These dramatic events and the dispute itself provoked a mass of litigation in the courts of Chancery and Star Chamber at Westminster. In the end Meighen won a partial victory, and Gittins was temporarily installed as second master in October 1612.

In fact, despite its popularity with the gentry and as a potential step towards the élite world of the universities and the Inns of Court, the school was not a remote institution. When ap Rees and Lacon scrapped with cudgels during their quarrel over the maypole, they used the fencing facilities at the school; and it was John Baker, the second master, who intervened when Lacon wanted to stop, and *'by force took the cudgel out of Hugh ap Rees' hand'*. Scholars were also employed to draw and witness

bonds for illiterate tradesmen. For instance, Richard Langley (whose father, a prosperous tailor, had purchased the abbey site after the Dissolution), could remember being asked by a cooper in 1566 to go to Alberbury to witness a bond, *'at what time he was a scholar in the free school of Shrewsbury'* aged about fifteen.

In many ways too the school was a microcosm of the town's daily life. Although their day ended a little earlier, the boys began work at much the same time - 7 a.m. in winter and 6 a.m. during the rest of the year, and their dinner break was also marked by the ringing of a bell. If the town had its own tradition of disorder on Election night (in which the schoolboys participated), so the school developed its own customary 'mischief nights'. The main holiday periods were also the same as those enjoyed by the town - Christmas, Easter and Whitsuntide. In addition, just as every householder was expected to attend church on the Sabbath and on holy days, so too were all the schoolboys who boarded with them. In practice then, townsfolk would have recognised in school life the same kind of close regulation that governed their own.

Service

Apart from the select few who went on to the universities at Oxford or Cambridge, or to study law at the Inns of Court, most lads, whether they had been to the school or not, would hope then to be taken into service as apprentices. Originally this had occurred at about the age of fifteen, or perhaps a little later if they came from outside town. By 1614 the Shearmen's company required their apprentices to be aged at least sixteen, and several of the other craft fellowships by that date would not allow their apprentices to become masters until they had reached the age of 24. Since the normal term of apprenticeship was seven years (long before this was made a legal requirement by statute in 1563), it is clear that sixteen was becoming the usual age to enter service, although some lads still began terms of eight to ten years, suggesting that they were younger than this.

If a lad came from a craft household where the father was still alive, he would normally be apprenticed to him, assuming he intended to follow the same occupation. Apprenticeships of this kind were not uncommon. Between 1588 and 1609, for example, about one fifth of apprentices registered by the Weavers' company were apprenticed to their fathers. In the Smiths'

The baker's apprentice (from a manuscript of 1596)

company the equivalent figure between 1622 and 1650 was more than one quarter. By contrast, orphaned or country lads had to look around for a master willing to take them on. This required local knowledge, especially as most crafts would not allow their masters to keep more than one apprentice until the sixth year of service, although the Drapers permitted two apprentices to be kept, and the Glovers three. It was here that the advice of friends and relatives living in town could prove useful. The experience of the London turner Nehemiah Wallington in the 1650s suggests that hopeful lads first went round the shops themselves asking for an interview. Subsequent negotiations would then involve the families concerned. On 24 August 1549 in Mardol, for example, in the presence of his father the tanner Thomas Clerke and other friends, Richard Clerke was apprenticed for seven years to the shearman John Heynes to learn the trade of shearing *'and also to be instructed in buying and selling of Welsh cloths'*. By 1626 the Shearmen's company also allowed masters to take on lads for a trial period of one month before deciding whether to register them with the craft.

When Thomas Phillips was apprenticed to his father the butcher John Phillips on 14 November 1622, the terms of the indentures were typical. He was to serve for seven years; to perform his master's business well and truly and to keep all necessary secrets; he was not to play dice, cards or other games, or to frequent taverns and alehouses except on his master's business. Sex was also strictly forbidden. Proverbially the lot of an apprentice was a harsh one and life in some households was undoubtedly tough. In 1582 the apprentice Sam Wisbecke wrote to his uncle begging him to tell the bailiffs about his plight: he was dressed in threadbare clothes, and his master and dame were putting it about that he was a common thief. The fate of Thomas Luntley in 1595 was also a wretched one. Taken on at the age of fourteen for a probationary period by the shoemaker Philip Wilding, he was accused of molesting his master's infant daughter. To force a confession Luntley was tied naked to a bed and brutally flogged, while a friend of Wilding's threatened to castrate him with a knife or pair of scissors.

All the same, craft records suggest that the number of apprentices who actually ran away was not great, although homesickness must have been common, especially in the early months of service. In 1547 after six months with a Shrewsbury weaver, William Medlycott went back to his grandparents' farm; and in 1594, a reverse case of a lad returning to Shrewsbury, Richard Leaton, apprenticed to Thomas Harley a London haberdasher in Fleet Street, returned home to his father who was living near the Welsh Bridge. Harley wrote to Leaton's father asking him to find out why his son had run away, *'and see what he can say whether both I and my wife did not both love him and tender him as our own child'*.

Maidservant, 1550

Maidservants were normally employed for a year at a time, usually for wages of about five to eight shillings, although food and lodgings of course were free. Their duties included cleaning (using sand to mop up grease and scour pans), cooking, putting children to bed, de-lousing their employers, and getting stuck in on the dreaded wash day. Household discipline could be strict. In 1508 the lawyer John Pole even sued his maidservant Elizabeth Plowden in the town court for losing some of his domestic utensils. Welsh girls were popular, although the experience of Margaret verch Howell in the 1590s reveals an ever-present risk. She complained that Edward, the son of her master the mercer Thomas Mytton, had got her pregnant and then broken a promise of marriage. Her master had shown little sympathy for her plight. The boy had been packed off to London to get him out of trouble, and she was now left on her own with a three month old baby to care for.

Conditions could be as bad for maidservants as apprentices. At midsummer 1575 Elizabeth Williams was taken on by the shoemaker Thomas ap Roger, but was poorly treated: there was little food and her master was behind with her wages. Three weeks before Christmas she took off and found another employer in the Abbey Foregate. Her old dame came over to take her back, and when Elizabeth refused, gave her a sound beating. Elizabeth took revenge by accusing the dame of cheating in business. Every week she had received twelve pounds of wool from Hugh Benion to spin into yarn for two shillings, some of which she craftily kept back for herself, sending the yarn to be woven into cloth which she then sold for her own profit.

Setting up shop

Once he had served his term, an apprentice could apply to be admitted as a freeman of his craft fellowship. Already by his last year in service he might be sufficiently competent to be entrusted with the shop, although he was still not allowed to set up in business. When about 1600 the master of the apprentice smith George Griffithes died leaving him with one more year still to serve, Griffithes hired the shop and tools from the widow and began trading himself - angering his company who later refused to admit him. Normally in such circumstances, arrangements were made to put the apprentice to another master to serve out his time.

In practice many apprentices never got as far as becoming a master. For example, of 103 apprentices registered in the Weavers' company between 1591 and 1609 only about 20 eventually became masters. In the Mercers' company, the rate of attrition was rather less. Some 51 apprentices were registered between 1573 and about 1586, of whom 24 were in due course admitted. In the Shearmen's company prospective masters were obliged to 'proffer' or notify their intention to become a master in the preceding year. Even at this late stage in service, many were still unable subsequently to set up their own shops. Of 94 shearmen who proffered in the decade after 1571, only about sixty eventually became masters.

Many factors could explain why apprentices never became masters in the crafts in which they had been registered. Some obviously died or ran away, or left to try their luck elsewhere. Many Shrewsbury masters, particularly before 1550, had in fact come from other towns. They obtained their freedom in the craft by the alternative method of purchase as a 'foreigner', paying a higher entry fine. Some apprentices, however, were simply attracted to other jobs. In the 1600s, for example, the apprentice weaver John ap Rees was struck from the register book because he had left his trade and become an ostler (stable lad) at one of the inns. But in many cases it was the difficulty in raising sufficient 'stock' or capital that prevented young men from setting up shop. This was obviously less of a problem for wealthy families. So long as male heirs continued to be produced, their businesses could persist for a long time, especially if supported by property investments. Big dyers like the Gardiners, for example, can be traced in the records over several generations, in their case eventually setting up as minor gentry at Sansaw. They were also landlords of the court

in Frankwell where Robert Davis and Widow Morris lived (see the previous chapter).

For those less fortunate, work would have to be secured, at least for a time, as a journeyman. Such men were often hired for the year, although, as we saw in chapter 1, they could be taken on for a shorter period like the busy weeks before Christmas. Work also piled up before Easter. In 1552 John Davis was hired by the tailor William Poyner to work for four weeks before Easter, splitting the profits between them. But Davis left after a fortnight leaving Poyner unable *to work and make such garments for his customers as he then did promise them so to do'*. The Weavers' company at least insisted on two weeks notice before a journeyman could leave. Eventually a few journeymen were able to save enough to take out their freedom. The shearman Abraham Griffiths made his 'proffer' in 1572, but had to work as a journeyman for five years before being admitted a master in 1578. Conversely the Glovers allowed any master who fell into poverty and found it impossible to maintain a shop, to hire out his labour to others.

Weaver's workshop, 1630

At the same time there was nothing to stop journeymen from travelling elsewhere to look for work. By the early seventeenth century, the Shearmen's company regularly gave penny doles to tramping artisans who had come to town.

Several of the crafts are known to have had separate fellowships for their journeymen. The records of the Weavers' company, for instance, show that their journeymen had their own officers and ordinances (kept in the company chest at their hall in Murivance). In 1475, in return for a contribution to the Weavers' service of Our Lady in St. Chad's, the company also agreed to find a hall in which the journeymen could keep their own sports and recreations over summer. Before the Reformation, these fellowships were also allocated places in the annual Corpus Christi procession, and as such were an integral part of the craft system.

Courtship and marriage

The age and length of service was one important reason why marriage took place quite late, typically in the mid to late twenties. Most men would get married about the time they set up shop - the dowry which the bride brought with her, in particular, was a valuable addition to the resources of the new household. But before then lads would be expected to show that they had the bearings to be quiet, hard-working husbands. The sort of behaviour which was unlikely to get approval is illustrated by the actions of draper apprentices at the start of the sixteenth century. At that time the Drapers were not the only company whose masters were seeking to make a living from the growth of the Welsh cloth trade. Other craftsmen from the Tailors', Mercers' and Shearmen's companies were also participating in the trade, much to the disgust of the draper apprentices who feared for their livelihood. In 1517 a group of them sought to use physical force to prevent other tradesmen from riding to the markets at Oswestry and Welshpool. The shearman George Spurstow was threatened in this way on Onslow Heath. Turning to the apprentice Mathew Piers, he told him *'me think ye be not wise*

to trouble us shearmen as ye do, for ye have nought. And as long as ye use this manner of fighting and waiting, no man will do for you. And if ye do well and soberly, men will be glad to levy [hire] *you and to marry their daughters unto you'.*

These lads must have been at the age to start courting. For youngsters coming from families of rich merchants, gentry or the 'quality', courtship was usually a pretty stilted affair. The large financial interests involved ensured that parents and influential kin, masters or patrons ('friends' as they were known) played an active role in negotiations, and courting itself was quite formal. Among the rest of the population, however, there was more scope for intimacy between couples. Very common was the practice known as bundling. Usually after they had exchanged promises of marriage, couples were allowed to spend the night together in bed. They kept most of their clothes on, and contact was limited to heavy petting. It was a good way for couples to discover how compatible they were without, it was hoped, risking pregnancy. No stigma was attached and mothers often took an active part in arranging a bundling for their daughters. In 1592, for example, Thomas Swaine who came from a farming family in Castle Foregate was courting Joan Rider from

Bundling on the truckle bed

Harlescott. Their relationship had been partly broken during Lent, but in May Swaine was asked to visit her again, *'whereupon he went thither and being late in the night they lay both together in their clothes upon a bed in the house'*, touching only their hands and faces.

Courtship usually ended in pledges of troth (mutual acceptance). These pledges were legally binding contracts although their status if unwitnessed was unclear. They were often accompanied by tokens of affection. In March 1553 at the Welsh Gate Thomas Bayly gave as tokens to his prospective wife Margaret a piece of gold known as a half angel; a handkerchief fringed with white lace; a gilt ring; and a pomander tied with a ribbon of black silk lace. (A pomander was a hollow case, often shaped like an apple or orange, containing perfume.) Margaret was obviously not too impressed: she broke her promise and married the minstrel William Petton instead. Popularly it was felt that a contract could be terminated provided compensation was paid. In 1552, for instance, Richard Hethe agreed to pay 13s 4d to a Chester girl whom he had promised to marry at Battlefield.

On her marriage, the family of the bride paid a dowry to the family of the groom. At his death one third of any freehold estate he may have accumulated would pass by law to the widow, although the wealthy could better this provision by settling property upon newly weds for their maintenance and for a future annuity or 'jointure' for the widow. It was also a Shrewsbury custom that one third of the goods and chattels of a deceased burgess would go to his children and two thirds to his wife and executors. So it was very difficult in considering marriage to separate love and money, and even poor couples with few resources might find the advice of 'friends' enough to discourage them.

A sad case in 1611 shows this well. In May 1608 the musician John Meyricke and Elizabeth Cherle from Wallop on the Long Mountain had privately pledged their troth; *'and so they continued lovers and friends together although they did not proceed to marriage but did defer the time of because their friends would not agree to their wedding'*. In July 1611 they reluctantly released each other from their promises, and Meyricke went to Shrewsbury to find work. Some days later he was playing his tabor and pipe in an alehouse in Frankwell when Elizabeth came in carrying on her head a pail of milk which she had brought to town to sell. It was distressing for them both, and they walked out together to the Welsh Bridge. He told her that he wanted to go for a swim, which may have been a veiled threat to drown himself because Elizabeth, *'knowing his intent would not permit him but laid fast hold about his neck and said "sweet John, you shall not"'*. So they turned back and found another alehouse in Frankwell, where Meyricke struck up music with a bagpiper, and Elizabeth danced with another old boyfriend. At 8 p.m. Meyricke turned in for bed, but Elizabeth went out for a walk and was later picked up by the watch and held over for the night. Next morning she returned to Meyricke's bedside and said her heart was broken. He told her to cheer up; perhaps they could still get wedded in church. She answered,

'John, it is too late; my heart is broken already'. They began to drink each other's health, but she was sick. Meyricke then went out to play at the sign of The Goat where Elizabeth later joined him, sitting sadly at the door. They visited other alehouses, but she started to drift in and out of consciousness. At last, asking God to forgive them both, and that Meyricke should *'see her honestly brought home'*, she died - probably of alcoholic poisoning.

Neither of them, certainly not Meyricke, would have been able to bring much to their marriage. They lived remote from the very rich, such as the great lawyer Richard Prynce who left in his will over £600 towards the marriages of each of his four legitimate daughters. Modest townsfolk had much less to give. In 1558 at Coleham the widow Elizabeth Wilcocks promised

A merchant's wedding (about 1500)

a dowry of £5 plus two cows and two heifers towards the marriage of her daughter Gwen, and other dowries for less than this are also known. Masters could also take care of the marriages of their maidservants. In 1559 the shearman John Aspley offered to pay his fellow shearman John Suker one half of all his goods and chattels, excepting one cow, and £4 in ready money if Suker would wed his servant Margaret. He also promised that Suker could move in and share his house until he (Aspley) died. He probably hoped that the couple would look after him in his old age.

By the seventeenth century marriage contracts without a formal wedding ceremony were increasingly frowned upon, although even then a ceremony in church was still not legally necessary. Couples could instead take part in a clandestine marriage. These were held in secret without prior reading of the banns, although they were still meant to be taken by a clergyman according to the rites of the Book of Common Prayer. In 1633, for example, John Powell, the minister of St. Julian's, married the tailor Richard Leech at a widow's house near St. Alkmund's in the presence of three witnesses. Leech abandoned his wife after a fortnight and allegedly entered a bigamous marriage at Lichfield. Accusations of this kind provided much of the business of the church courts.

For most young masters in one of the town's craft fellowships a clandestine marriage would have been unthinkable. A formal church wedding, usually at the church door, set a seal on the marriage contract and publicly demonstrated the creation of a new craft household. In Shrewsbury, as elsewhere, it was compulsory for masters to attend the weddings of fellow brethren in their company. The Weavers even required the membership to attend the weddings of their journeymen, and by the 1590s typically contributed bottles of sack (sherry) to the wedding feast.

Companies and guilds

Including the Millers based in the Abbey Foregate, there existed
sixteen craft fellowships in Tudor Shrewsbury, although there
were of course many more trades than that - 36 are recorded in
the burgess admissions between 1500 and 1550. The fellowships,
or companies as they were usually called, were in fact
amalgamations of different trades. The Saddlers' company,
for instance, included glaziers, painters, plumbers, lorimers
and spurriers. The Carpenters and Tilers included joiners,
sawyers and bricklayers, although the joiners were later united
in 1568 with the Fletchers', Bowyers' and Coopers' company.
The Mercers' company was perhaps the most miscellaneous:
it contained mercers, hosiers, ironmongers, goldsmiths,
pewterers, grocers, apothecaries, button makers, purse makers,
brass-founders and cappers, and later upholsterers, hatters and
stationers as well. This grouping of trades under distinct craft
fellowships had been official government policy since the 1360s.
For every tradesman there ought ideally be a fellowship to which
he should belong. After 1436-7 the rules drawn up by these
companies also had to be certified by the assize judges or local
justices of the peace. The craft system in fact was an artificial
means of imposing organization upon town society, making it
easier for the authorities to rule.

Today these companies are usually described as 'guilds'.
But in the sixteenth century that term was applied more narrowly
to bodies that were mutual benefit societies with religious
functions, often incorporated for that purpose. In that sense,
only three guilds, so-called, are known in Tudor Shrewsbury -
the Drapers' guild of the Holy Trinity, the Mercers' guild of St.
Michael the Archangel, and the guild of St. Winifred,
incorporated in 1487, which was a select guild of the élite
of Shrewsbury and the Abbey Foregate together with their wives.
Before the Reformation four other companies are also known
to have maintained altars and paid priests to sing masses for
their dead, although they were described not as guilds but as
'fraternities'.

Seal of the Drapers' Guild

Seal of St. Winifred's Guild

In the case of the Drapers' and Mercers' guilds, it was possible
to become a member without being in trade and still enjoy the
benefits of the guild, including the prayers of their priest and of
the almspeople. A good example was the admission of Fulk Colle
to the Mercers' guild in 1528-9, *'taken in only to have the prayer
of the priest and poor people and to go yearly in procession on
Corpus Christi day and not to trade'*. The Colles (or Coles)
were an old family of town gentry who had extensive property
in the county. In Shrewsbury their interests included a mill and
several acres of land in Frankwell adjacent to the tiny hospital
of St. John with which they were closely associated.

By 1564 the hospital was sometimes known as Cole's
almshouses although it was not until 1590 that John Colle
actually purchased the premises. The family itself lived in Colle
Hall off Knockyn Street (Hill's Lane) on a plot including
a private chapel and an orchard which overlooked Doglane
(Claremont Street). For a gentleman such as Fulk Colle

Remains of Colle Hall, 19th century

membership of the Mercers' guild was a useful way of socializing with other important townsmen. In theory such guilds were dissolved in 1547-8 and their properties confiscated by the Crown, but there were loopholes in the Act which the Drapers managed to exploit to retain their lands.

All the companies were organized under wardens, assistants and stewards. Most craftsmen in their lifetime could expect to serve in one of the junior offices at least, while the fortunate would eventually join the ranks of the most senior brethren or 'aunciency'. The regulations of the companies laid down the procedure for craft elections, auditing the accounts and holding festival days. In addition trades were demarcated and terms of apprenticeship specified, as well as the number of shops and journeymen allowed. Usually only one shop was permitted, although the Mercers allowed another shop for hardware and, like the Glovers, a second 'show' during the fairs. The companies also supervised honest dealing and proper workmanship through a system of searchers. In 1507, for

example, the wardens of the shoemakers presented two masters to the bailiffs for shoddy shoes made of horse leather. Within six months of their election the wardens and sitters (assistants) of the Weavers' company also had to measure all the warp bars of the brethren to ensure that they were of uniform length (1609), while the Glovers carried out a monthly search for inferior wares (1614). The Mercers also periodically called in weights and measures to the company hall beside the Sextry tavern to be checked and sealed.

But the importance of the craft fellowships in the running of the economy should not be exaggerated. About one fifth of working adult males were 'out of craft', and there was much overlapping of trades. Many basic tasks too such as spinning, thread-making, and knitting were done informally in households scattered throughout the town - as the case of Elizabeth Williams, mentioned before, illustrates. Women's labour, in particular, although scarcely recognized in craft records, was often essential in the workshop (for example in sewing skins and gloves), and they were mainly responsible for hawking fish, bread and dairy produce from door to door.

Companies in fact had a role more like the 'houses' of a boarding school. Although many people work in such schools who do not belong to a house, it is these groupings that represent the face of the school and through which it is run. In the same way the companies in Tudor Shrewsbury were used as the groups to levy important taxes; to muster troops and supply soldiers for the militia; to find beds and furnishings for the assize judges and the Council in the Marches; to raise money for the Whitsun plays; to supply warders who patrolled the fairs; and (by the seventeenth century) to maintain buckets and ladders in case of fire. Above all, in the old Corpus Christi procession the companies paraded behind their banners as the official representation of the town. In fact, before the Reformation keeping procession in due order was perhaps their most important concern, as ordinances show. The Tailors' and Skinners' combined company, for example, met annually six weeks before Corpus Christi at the Grey Friars at 7 a.m. to discuss what arrangements to make that year. Twenty tapers were kept ready, weighing 8 pounds each, and the stewards were responsible for choosing the colour of the livery and whether gowns and hoods should be worn. As with all the companies, half of all the fines imposed on the brethren for breaches of company rules was also diverted to the upkeep of the tapers, while the other half was paid to the bailiffs as representatives of the Crown.

As disputes over the order of procession show, Corpus Christi could provide craftsmen with a strong sense of identity with their company. This was reinforced by fraternal obligations, including attendance at the marriages and burials of craft brethren. The Weavers required all their masters to be present at the *'knell gatherings'* of deceased brethren or their wives, and by 1625 they kept a black cloth for the occasion, 3 1/4 yards in length and 2 yards broad, which was spread over the hearse. The Shearmen too regularly spent money at the *'eating of*

a mort', and these wakes were sometimes attended by prominent townsmen and other gentlemen.

Another important occasion for craft solidarity, at least before the rise of firearms, was archery practice at the butts on Kingsland. Near these butts the companies maintained their own arbours (mentioned in 1528), while the Corvisors also laid out a maze or 'race', first heard of in 1565. Before practising the companies were meant to mark out the limits of the shooting range for safety, and both the Drapers and the Smiths were fined in 1543 for failing to do this. This shows that the archers aimed not only at targets, but also took part in contests known as over-shot or rovers, where the aim was to fire an arrow as far as possible. A day out with the company on a Saturday afternoon in summer, resting in the shade of the arbour, was the perfect way to relax - helped, naturally, by a few pints of Shrewsbury beer. In 1584 the Shearmen spent 26s 8d at John Hassold's alehouse or inn (equivalent to about 960 pints of beer, although food would also have been bought), *'that day the company went to Kingsland to shoot over-shot'*.

Chapter 5 - Presentments and Neighbours

The Great Court

Great Court meal

Tudor Shrewsbury was a tightly regulated society, in some ways like a boarding school or a regiment. One of the most important institutions used to control behaviour was the Great Court or 'court leet', held twice a year in spring and autumn. On each occasion a check was taken of all the male householders who owed 'suit' of court, probably either in the Guildhall or in the open air in the Cornmarket, during which selected men were also sworn in as the constables responsible for keeping order in the streets in which they lived. Either before or after the review the bailiffs and their six assistants or 'sessors' shared a hearty meal. In the early sixteenth century it once consisted of bread and ale, beef and mutton, eight geese and three pigs, garnished with salt, butter, vinegar and spices. The cook was paid 8d for his labour.

Before the court day, lists of the householders who had to attend were prepared for each street or suburb by the town clerk or his assistants in rectangular paper books. Attendance marks were then placed beside each name on the day itself. These indicated whether the householder had been present or had obtained permission to be absent; whether he was ill or out of town; whether he had left or died since the last court; or whether he had simply failed to turn up, in which case he would have to pay a small fine of 6d. Suit lists were normally kept up for a few years before a new paper book was purchased. In the meantime, those who had died or gone would be crossed out and the names of newcomers, or 'new streeters' as they were called, were inserted. A householder could also be replaced by another male member of his household if he had died or was incapacitated by age, provided the substitute was old enough.

In the first half of the sixteenth century attendance was quite high and only about one tenth of male householders were normally fined for failing to appear without an excuse. But afterwards residents became increasingly reluctant to attend. By 1600 the proportion of those fined was about one quarter, rising further to one third by 1620. The old sense of collective responsibility was beginning to decay, a process which became especially marked after 1660.

The lists of male householders were also used to draw up names of potential jurymen from which the Great Inquest was selected and sworn. In the fifteenth century the number of jurors so sworn was 12, but in later years it could vary between 15 and 20. It was the task of the Great Inquest, sitting in the Guildhall, to sift through the accusations and complaints, known as presentments, which had been entered beforehand by the inhabitants, and decide which were true and which could not be proved. The inquest itself usually met several days after the Great Court. At some point during its deliberations, the inquest also enjoyed a meal paid for by the town. In 1599, for example, the jurors spent eight shillings at an alehouse run by the weaver Hugh Gittins. By that date, however, it was rare for prominent citizens to serve on an inquest - an important change since the early sixteenth century, and another sign of how the Great Court was beginning to lose its significance in the community.

In 1495 some forty townships were added to the eight townships that had anciently comprised Shrewsbury's rural liberties, and these new hamlets were also drawn into the jurisdiction of the Great Court, although they were given a separate Great Inquest to deal with their own presentments. All the same, their male householders still owed appearance at the Great Court in Shrewsbury. Not surprisingly, this was much resented. For the men in Clive, for example, the most northerly of these townships, it meant a round trip of fifteen miles. In 1529-30 the townships asked unsuccessfully if, instead of a *'whole appearance'*, only five men from each community need attend as had been their own practice before 1495.

Streeters' bills

Presentments were made in three ways. First, they could be drawn up by the constables themselves. Secondly, they could be brought by private individuals. To do this the aggrieved party could go at any time to the bailiffs and swear or 'depose' on oath, preferably supported by witnesses, that he or she had been harmed in some way (usually during a fight). A record of this deposition was then kept by the town clerk, and in due course submitted to the Great Inquest. But the most common presentments were those made by the male householders in each street or suburb, known as streeters. Some weeks before the Great Court, the town clerk's office would prepare small sheets of paper called bills, headed with the name of the street and the date of the court. These bills were then sent out to selected residents, and word was passed about that the streeters should meet to draw up their presentments on the bill. In 1633 for instance, the shoemaker Francis Fisher was instructed to summon the Dogpole streeters to meet next Thursday between 3 and 4 p.m. In theory, failure to attend the making of the streeters' bill was itself a presentable offence, although the obligation was not strictly enforced. In medieval Shrewsbury these gatherings had been known as Little Inquests, although by Tudor times this description was no longer used.

Having selected one of their number who could write, the streeters would discuss which incidents and nuisances ought to be presented, and these were then written down upon the bill. In 1621 David Lloyd ap Roger of Frankwell even took the opportunity to get a presentment put down against Richard Owen for calling him nicknames at the meeting itself, *'before the whole street'*. Once the bill had been completed, it was sent back to the Exchequer where it was gathered together with all the other bills, and in due course handed over to the Great Inquest for perusal. The bills were then annotated with the Inquest's verdict and returned to the town clerk's office. A list of fines was then drawn up on an 'estreat' roll or book, and instructions went out to the three sergeants to collect the fines in their wards. Because cash was often scarce, domestic items were sometimes handed over, valued and then sold off instead. In 1545 these included pieces of cloth, a brass mortar, a gown edged with fox fur, a pair of clothworker's shears, and other pots and utensils. Those who could not pay were imprisoned, and, as we have seen, this often led to a petition to be released.

Alesellers and swine-keepers were always presented. Although in theory these presentments were entered for breaking town regulations, they were in effect a simple form of licensing. The same was true of the hawkers presented for regrating (buying up produce to sell at a profit) and forestalling the markets, especially those for fish and butter. Such offences were only regarded as serious in dearth years when provisions were in short supply. Otherwise the most important group of presentments were those dealing with fights, known as affrays and bloods, breaches of market regulations, and nuisances - such as timber stacked in the street, unmuzzled dogs, noisy pigs, reeking latrines and the dumping of weeds in the churchyards or other people's gardens. In 1552, for example, Mr. Dawes was presented by the Wyle Cop for a *'jakes'* - a jake house or privy - near the Grey Friars, *'the more rather a poison and a very filthy poison indeed, and too bad to be suffered in any town to poison men withall'*. Cleaning out latrines or 'heaving houses' was organized privately, and it is clear from the presentments that St. Mary Waterlode and the other postern gates were traditionally used as dumps for excrement and other domestic waste. The public latrines of four stools erected on the Stone Bridge in 1564, like those built on the Welsh Bridge in 1581 *'for the necessary easement of strangers'*, used a more acceptable mode of disposal - straight into the river itself. The municipal dung heap in Roushill lane could also be used to dispose of waste. In 1580 it was let to the draper John Dawes for 30 shillings a year on condition that he did not use *'iron bound'* carts (i.e. with iron strips on the wheel rims) to carry the dung away across the bridges - presumably to protect the road surfaces. Another spot for disposing of muck was the 'spout hole' outside the postern gate at Austin Friars. In later centuries it became notorious as the 'mudholes', and marked the outfall of an ancient stream that had once flowed from a post-glacial bog on the site of the Cornmarket. (Gullet Passage is thought to record part of its course.) In 1530-1 the streeters of both Romaldesham and Claremont presented the coroners for failing to repair the town wall *'which is fallen to decay at the end of the spout'*.

The coroners in fact were often presented for the shoddy state of the town fabric whose upkeep was their responsibility. In 1530, for example, the streeters of Corvisors Row complained that the street or 'pavement' near the High Cross was so broken up that carts were likely to overturn and oxen to break their legs. They also pointed out a ruined chimney *'that stand in peril of*

falling on your children'. Such fears were sometimes justified. In 1536 a maltman had just pitched his load in the market and was tying up his horse in Grope Lane when an old chimney collapsed and killed him.

Presentments were also the simplest way to take action against anti-social neighbours, like William Hekyn, presented by the Shoplatch streeters in 1536 as *'a goer in the night, barking under his neighbours' walls'*; or Katherine Hopton of Knockyn Street, presented in the same year for crapping in a bowl and leaving it outside her neighbours' doors; or William Harryes, privately presented about 1610 by his neighbour James Tomson for keeping a sty right beside his chamber. The pigs were squealing day and night, and their waste was seeping beneath the wall and under his bed, threatening to infect his family with disease.

The gumblestool

Women presented as scolds could either be ducked in water using the gumblestool (new ones were built in 1518 and 1669), or were led around town wearing a bridle (mentioned in by-laws of 1638). Pimping was also regulated. In 1527 Howell ap Edenevet was presented for keeping a brothel in Frankwell, as was Edith Wancker of Coleham in 1586. In 1552 the Knockyn streeters complained that Richard Nichols was keeping six women in a tenement there, probably for the same purpose. Earlier in 1535 they had also begged the bailiffs to have the prostitute Elizabeth, *'the friars' wife'*, thrown out of the street. These were all poor areas, where prostitution offered a way to scrape a living.

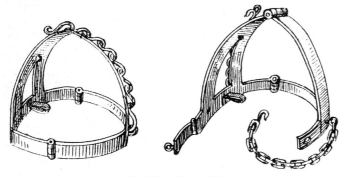

The Shrewsbury bridle

Affrays and bloods

If the Great Inquest found that a presentment for a brawl was true, the offender would be fined 3s 4d for the affray or 6s 8d if blood had been drawn. Even the most trivial incidents might have to be considered as in 1593 when the Knockyn streeters presented a tanner's wife for pinching the ear of a little boy and causing it to bleed. Often the inquest would not be able to come to any conclusion. In 1537-8, for example, 57 incidents were reported but only 24 of them led to a fine. The number of these fines increased four-fold in the 70 years after 1550 as the population began to grow. Many fights involved drinkers, apprentices and housewives, but sometimes even important citizens could be presented.

A good example occurred on Friday, 8 March 1589. A respected shearman, Humphrey Anderton, had just died and arrangements had been made to bear his corpse from the Abbey Foregate to St. Mary's for burial. Among those who gathered beforehand with the wardens of the Shearmen's company in the Abbey Foregate were Alderman Richard Owen (who built Owen's Mansion in the High Street in 1592) and Anderton's landlord, the great lawyer Richard Prynce. The cortège then set out across the Stone Bridge, with the coffin being carried ahead and the mourners following on behind. As they climbed the Wyle, they reached a well known inn called the Red Lion. As property deeds and other evidence shows, this was the same establishment as that known simply as the Lion (now the Lion Hotel). At the Red Lion other aldermen were waiting to join the procession, including Robert Ireland, the nephew of Robert Ireland senior, of Shrewsbury and Lythwood (died 1583), whom we have mentioned before. The younger Ireland's father, Thomas, had also become a prosperous merchant and had purchased a country estate at Albrighton, four miles north of Shrewsbury, where his branch of the family resided until the eighteenth century. After some jostling for position, Robert Ireland teamed up with Prynce and Owen. The three of them then walked up Dogpole abreast, occasionally stepping over the open drain which ran down the middle of the street.

Arms of Ireland of Albrighton

Near the middle of the Drapers' almshouses on the western edge of St. Mary's churchyard, a large stone stuck out into the street - perhaps a block for mounting horses. Both Ireland and Prynce were walking on that side of the street, with Prynce himself beside the wall. It seemed that Prynce would have to step behind Ireland and allow him to go on ahead.

The Drapers' almshouses

Suddenly, as they approached the stone, Prynce darted forward to get in front. But Ireland was ready for him. What happened then took place so quickly that no witness was able to give a clear account. Owen, who was on the other side of the street, was holding a handkerchief to his nose because of the smell from the drain; when he looked up he saw the two men shouldering and barging each other. Others, like the widow Elizabeth Scott who was sewing by her door, saw Prynce stagger back with blood flowing from his head. The pall bearer Richard Hardinge, hearing the commotion, helped set the coffin down in the road, and turned round to see Ireland dagger in hand, his glove smeared with blood. Both Prynce and Ireland had a servant with them who rushed in to help their masters, whipping out their own daggers and striking out at each other.

Ireland was pulled into an adjoining house by his brother George as Prynce screamed, *'let me not be murdered for I have never a weapon upon me'*. Afterwards the bailiffs took down depositions from the witnesses. Some weeks later the Great Inquest then looked over the evidence, and Ireland was fined 6s 8d for a blood. The reluctance by both Prynce and Ireland to give way by the almshouses shows how touchy individuals were about their status. This sensitivity was also reflected in the practice known as 'taking the wall'. When people walked down the street, they tried to keep to the wall side and force others of inferior status, coming from the other direction, to step towards the middle where the drain was. The shearman John Pewe was once imprisoned for disrespect towards Richard Hardinge, then one of the wardens of the Shearmen's company and a pall bearer at Anderton's funeral, *'in taking the wall of him and jostling him in the passing by'*.

The brawl between Prynce and Ireland also illustrates how common it was for men to carry daggers. They were used mainly for eating, not as weapons. Cutlery did not become common until much later - in Shropshire about the eighteenth century. Until then the short dagger or knife was used to cut up food and pick it up with the point.

Knives only at the table

Various taboos were linked to the dagger's use, such as pointing it at your own face. As Caxton's *Book of Courtesy* put it: *'Bear not your knife toward your visage, for therein is peril and mickle* [much] *dread'*. Conversely, it was good manners, if you wanted to pass someone a knife, to take the point in your hand and offer him the handle.

We can see how knife pointing was used as a gesture of threat in an incident in 1516 involving Alderman Thomas Trentham junior (elected bailiff in 1512 and 1516) and the draper William Gittyns. Both men were in dispute over some property outside the Castle Gates, and Gittyns had begun a lawsuit in the court of Chancery at Westminster. On 28 May he was drinking with some friends in a parlour in the Gullet tavern between 8 and 9 p.m. when Trentham entered. *'God speed masters'*,

he said, to which they replied *'Welcome master Trentham'*. The alderman walked over to Gittyns and clapped him on the back: *'Gittyns, art thou here?'*. *'Yea sir'*, Gittyns answered, *'that I am'*. Trentham then reminded him of the lawsuit, but the draper countered that he hoped that the case would not get between them. *'Thou art a good fellow'*, said Trentham, sitting down at the table and ordering a quart of wine. *'William Gittyns'*, he went on, *'I have marvelled why thou wouldst accuse me and impeach* [sue] *me at London, and say so ill of me as it is told to me. I never gave thee any such cause'*. Gittyns then changed tack. Trentham was misinformed, he said. He had thought of bringing a lawsuit in London, but his friends had persuaded him against it. At this moment Trentham drew out his dagger, holding the point towards Gittyns's face. Then slowly he turned the blade point down to the board. *'By god's blood'*, he said, *'if I knew for certain that thou had impeached me at London, the one of us should never depart hence in god's health'*. He then took up his dagger again and sheathed it. Gittyns had now had enough. He got up, muttering that he wasn't going to stay to be murdered. As he moved off, Trentham grabbed him by the shirt, but Gittyns pulled away, ripping his shirt and jacket, and walked out into the street.

Peace bonds

Gittyns was right to fear Trentham, a notorious bully, said to maintain a gang of craftsmen, mostly from the leather-working trades, to intimidate his opponents. He also had powerful connections. He was related by marriage to the Corbets of Moreton Corbet, and had served under the Earl of Shrewsbury during the French campaign in 1513. Both his sons also made their careers working in the royal household. To seek protection from such a man in the local community was not easy. But in many other cases it was possible to get protection by turning to the bailiffs for help and asking for a peace bond.

The process was simple and was often used. A person in fear of harm appeared before the bailiffs and swore under oath that he or she was in danger of life or limb, and that the party who posed the threat ought to be bound over to keep the peace. A warrant was then issued and the accused, if found, was bound over with sureties - usually two in number, but sometimes more. At Michaelmas 1517 the merchant David Ireland sought the peace against the draper Thomas Knight who was then bound over in the sum of £40. He had three sureties, including two other drapers, who were each bound in the sum of £20 that Knight would fulfil the conditions of the bond.

The accused could either be obliged to keep the peace generally, or to keep the peace towards a specific individual. Normally the bond would last until a future sitting of the Small Court or the next Shrewsbury sessions. It could then be renewed, but more commonly the person who had been bound over was then discharged. In a small town it was easy to keep an eye on neighbours who had entered into a bond, and the system was both quite efficient and popular. As the Ireland case shows, even the most important citizens were sometimes involved - both Ireland and Knight were at different times elected bailiff. Nor did people feel that domestic and family disputes should be kept from the authorities. In January 1581, for example, Beatrix Hosier sought the peace against her own husband, and in May 1592 the gentleman Edward Higgons was bound over to keep the peace towards his brother Richard, a tanner by trade and also one of the attorneys in the Small Court. In the Higgons case, a family quarrel was simmering over an allegation that Edward had pinched a branched candlestick. In the preceding November Richard himself had been bound over on condition that he and his family would keep the peace towards Edward and his family.

The most dramatic family clash, however, involved the Colles of Colle Hall. On 14 October 1555 Fulk Colle and his elder step-brother Robert were separately bound over to keep the peace towards each other. Their quarrel probably involved the inheritance of property. Robert's father had died in the previous year, and was alleged to have made a death bed declaration to his second wife that Robert was an illegitimate son, which

would have ruled out his succession to Colle Hall. At any rate, the bonds in this case proved a spectacular failure. Within a day or two Robert was violently assaulted by his step-brother at the family home. Grabbing a pike to defend himself he smashed Fulk beneath the eye and killed him. He was then arrested, bound over and later indicted for murder at the sessions in July 1556, eventually securing a royal pardon for having acted in self defence.

Peace bonds were sought by individuals, but it was also possible for townsfolk to gang up as a group against an obnoxious neighbour. A good example was the action taken against Thomas Hatton in September 1593. Members of Hatton's family

Hatton's Mansion

had originally been glovers in the Abbey Foregate, but since 1547 they had built up a business on the Rea Brook at Sutton Lower Mill, becoming minor gentry in the process. Thomas himself had been one of the wardens of the Millers' company in 1590. He was an evil man, fiercely protective of what he took to be his property, *'who careth not in his rage whom nor how he striketh'* as his neighbours complained. Several times he had assaulted residents in the Foregate, using either a cudgel, a dagger, an iron chisel or a paddle. He was also alleged to have killed or maimed fifteen swine belonging to poor Widow Shutt whose house and backyard adjoined his, a large timber-framed house which stood on the edge of the suburb (near the site of the Column). At harvest time Hatton had also attacked several poor people working in the common field with a *'terrible, sharp briar'*, specially cut to hand, and had threatened to shoot with his crossbow two servants who were pulling down some enclosures which he had erected on the commons. With the same weapon he had fired bolts into his neighbours' sheep and pigs. Supported by depositions taken from fifteen Foregate residents, including Widow Shutt and her daughter, a number of accusations against Hatton were made to the bailiffs. He bluntly refused to be bound over to keep the peace, so the bailiffs committed him to prison, *'there to remain until he conformed himself in that behalf'*.

Drains and rights of way

The Great Inquest could also be called upon to adjudicate in disputes between neighbours. An example has already been mentioned in Chapter 3 when the jurymen investigated the claim that a new house in Shoplatch had blocked an ancient water course. Another case occurred in 1560-1 when the Great Inquest came over to Frankwell to inspect the way rainwater ran off the house of the glover Roger Nettylls and onto his ground. According to Nettylls, his neighbour John Balle, another glover, had diverted the rainwater from its *'common course'*, a claim which the Great Inquest endorsed. Balle paid little attention, however, and Nettylls was forced to bring a private lawsuit in the town court for damages. In coming to a decision the jurors relied upon the memory of old people who could remember how things had been in the past. In the Shoplatch case, for instance, three weavers were called to the scene to recall the path of the watercourse through the backyards over thirty years before. The verdict of the Great Inquest was then returned to the bailiffs, and appropriate action taken to rectify the nuisance.

A detailed picture of an inquest of this kind comes from a case in 1608. An ancient right of way ran from Nobold to a meadow which the farmer William Benyon rented from Thomas Berrington of Moat Hall. The path ran through another meadow called Cockshutt leasow, owned by Thomas Mackworth of a well known local family, with branches at Betton Strange and Meole Brace, which had sold to the corporation the land on which the Conduit Head was sited. Mackworth had recently planted some hedges across the path, preventing Benyon from getting easy access to his meadow. He complained to the bailiffs who instructed the Great Inquest to go and view the site. Fifteen inquest men were available, including five weavers, a smith, a mercer, a shearman, and a baker.

Since Mackworth's meadow lay within the old liberties, it was the town inquest and not that of the new liberties which was involved. On Thursday 8 December the jurymen, average age about fifty, walked out to the spot where they were met by Mackworth, Benyon and four old local farmers whom Benyon had brought along as witnesses. Mackworth himself had brought none, and at first angrily told the inquest to get off his land, but he was taken aside and gently persuaded to let them wander around the field. Benyon's witnesses were then sworn on oath and their evidence noted down by the mercer Evan Lloyd. The group then adjourned, minus Mackworth, to Benyon's farm where his maidservant had been preparing dinner. At the table the evidence given by the witnesses was read back to them, and the jurymen were asked one by one by the foreman to state whether they were agreed. They then broke up, some going over to Mackworth's house where they had been invited for a drink, and others returning to Shrewsbury. One of the jurors had recently had a bad fall and was by now feeling pretty stiff, so Benyon lent him a horse and accompanied the party back to the juror's alehouse in town. On Saturday, what was said to be a verdict on paper in Benyon's favour was handed over to the town clerk's assistant in the Exchequer, although it was later claimed that no definite verdict had in fact been reached; and that in any case such a verdict ought to have been certified as was custom by the whole inquest in the bailiffs' presence.

Chapter 6 - Going to law

The Small Court

Today it is unusual for private individuals to end up in court in civil matters, such as the recovery of debts, unless they are self-employed. Most litigation of this kind involves firms and limited companies. In Tudor Shrewsbury, however, most traders and craftsmen still worked on their own account, although some cloth merchants had begun to form partnerships by 1600. This was one reason why going to law was quite a normal part of daily life. During two years in the 1520s about one half of all male householders appeared as plaintiffs in the Shrewsbury court dealing with civil litigation, known as the Small Court, and two thirds as either plaintiffs or defendants.

It was possible to sue somebody at the central law courts at Westminster, provided the value of the case was over forty shillings, but cheaper and perfectly adequate justice could also be had locally at the Small Court. The great majority of lawsuits in Shrewsbury were for sums smaller than forty shillings, and so in any case had to be heard there. The Small Court could deal with disputes or transactions that had taken place within the liberties of the town, even though the parties may have come from outside. In 1521, for example, the vicar of Weobley in Herefordshire sued the vicar of Leominster for detaining a clerical tippet (cape) and other items, and also for a loan of 10 shillings. Both the delivery and the loan must have been made at Shrewsbury. Originally the court had met every other Tuesday in the Guildhall. But with the growth of population and trade a great litigation boom began after 1560. Within the next thirty years the number of lawsuits more than doubled, and to

accommodate the increase in business the town court began to meet weekly after 1586, a move already proposed by the borough council in 1577. From 1586 the Small Court also absorbed cases from the Abbey Foregate which until then had kept its own Great and Small Courts, probably in the handsome timber-framed building in Merivale (on the turning to Gay Meadow), which was known apparently as The Court House.

At least one of the two bailiffs always had to preside over the court. That led to a unique incident on Tuesday, 13 June 1592. Bailiff Ireland was out of town, but the other, Richard Powell, a rich merchant who later served as sheriff of Shropshire in 1594, was lying sick at home. To get him to court he was gently lifted onto a chair and carried through the streets to the Guildhall. After business had finished he was carried back again. By this date the actual legal pleadings were done out of court, and were monitored by the town clerk's office in the Exchequer. The court itself, when sitting, dealt mainly with trials and procedural matters. Most bailiffs, of course, were not trained in the law, but if a difficult legal point arose, they could get advice from their recorder, usually a prominent local barrister or judge.

Powell arms

The majority of lawsuits (actions) were brought to recover debts. Cases involving sales credit in particular were very common because it was unusual to pay on the nail. A good example was the action brought by the mercer Richard Hoode against Richard Banaster, Esq., of Hadnall. In November 1554 at his shop in the High Street Hoode sold over thirty shillings worth of groceries, haberdashery and other wares. No payment had since been made, so Hoode began a lawsuit in the Small Court. The transaction in this case was a large one, involving items such as pepper, cloves, saffron, ginger, dates and sugar; soap and starch; cloths and ribbons; knives, thread, bundles of yarn and a purse. It was obvious that Banaster's wife had put in a big order for herself and the household, including a 'paste', a popular type of female head-dress built up of pasteboard. But many other cases were for much smaller sums than this, sometimes for just a few pence. In many ways, bringing a debt action in the Small Court was rather like presenting a final demand, and in the majority of cases the defendants quietly paid up without further ado.

There were other kinds of lawsuits, including actions for breach of contract (to build a chimney, for example, or to full some cloth), poor workmanship, defamation and a miscellaneous group called 'trespass'. Actions for trespass could involve personal assault, allowing your livestock to break into someone else's land, harrying animals with dogs, or removing property. In 1508, for example, the draper John Lloyd sued Hugh Davies of Shelton for trespass because his pigs had got into Lloyd's barn and destroyed his mown wheat. It was also possible for masters to bring an action for trespass if for some reason they had lost the labour of their servants. In 1516 William Growte sued three men for sinking his servant's coracle after he had gone boating on Candlemas holiday in February. Presumably his servant had been off work since his ducking.

Process and tickets

A plaintiff usually began a lawsuit by notifying his intention to the town clerk's office. The office would then instruct the under-officers of the court to locate the defendant and serve either a writ of summons or of attachment to appear at the next court day. In the liberties this serving of process was done by the constables, but in town it was normally entrusted either to the sergeants or to individuals who had built up an intimate knowledge of where people lived. Many attorneys in the town court began their careers by doing that kind of work. Defendants who were summoned were simply informed of the need to appear. But if they were attached, they would have to find pledges or sureties, usually two in number, who were made responsible for their appearance. If defendants did not then come to the next court, they or their pledges could either be arrested or have some of their goods distrained (seized) to ensure their appearance. But defendants who lived outside the liberties and

Entering credit in the shop book

who had come to Shrewsbury for the day, could be distrained immediately. This procedure was often used against farmers and other traders coming to market. They might, for example, have their horses, pack-saddles, livestock or sacks of corn seized by the court officers.

If defendants were found, the under-officers had to inform the town clerk's office within two months, otherwise the case was discontinued. By the sixteenth century this information was then used to enter the action in a court book. Originally the under-officers had told the town clerk that process had been served by word of mouth. But this sometimes led to misunderstandings and actions being entered in the court books by mistake. To prevent this, 'tickets' began to be used. A ticket was a slip of paper or parchment, handed to the under-officer, on which a brief note of the parties and the nature of the action was written. Having served process on the defendant, the officer returned the ticket with a note added to that effect. The use of these tickets became the usual way of getting a lawsuit started.

The old Court House (right) in Merivale, 1800

Once they had appeared in court, not necessarily in person but normally through an attorney, defendants were traditionally

allowed three court days to answer the plaintiff - although a failure to answer on any of these days still led to a small fine unless a permit or 'essoin' was first obtained. If an answer had still not been received by the fourth court day, the plaintiff won. By then, however, many defendants would already have settled out of court, often at the moment they were first approached by the under-officer. A small fine of about 4d was payable for these 'concords' and that would be returned to the Exchequer and placed in a bag with all the other court receipts.

Saving harmless

Pledges were liable not only for the appearance of defendants in court but also for any sums awarded at the end of the lawsuit against the defendants which they then found they could not pay. But the pledges were usually promised beforehand that they would be indemnified for any losses they might incur, a practice known as 'saving harmless'. In 1574 the butcher John Gyttyns was sued by Richard Owen for the sum of 16s 6d. Gyttyns promised to save Richard Capper harmless if Capper would become one of his pledges. Subsequently Owen recovered the sum in dispute in the town court, and Capper was obliged to pay the sum as Gyttyns's pledge. On this occasion, however, Gyttyns failed to keep his promise, so Capper was forced to bring his own lawsuit against him.

In another case in January 1571 the under-officer David Nettles himself was asked by the butcher Thomas Ryton to stand as a pledge for the defendant Katherine Carter, promising to save him harmless at the same time. Katherine lost the suit, which had been brought by a Shrewsbury shearman, and a judgement of 20 shillings was awarded against her. She was not able to pay, so the court issued a writ of *capias* (arrest) against Nettles as her pledge - an arrest being the quickest way to obtain payment. When the sergeant Gilbert Wood arrived with the writ, Nettles persuaded him to go together to Ryton's shop in Butcher Row, where he told Ryton what had happened. The butcher then replied;

'Sergeant Gilbert, I pray you do not use any extremity against David Nettles for I must well discharge David for that capias as concerning Katherine Carter, for he the said David did stand surety at my request and for that matter I will save him harmless'.

On Ryton's promise to pay off the debt within a few days, the sergeant then agreed not to imprison Nettles but to leave Ryton instead under house arrest, supervised either by his sister or, in her absence, by his wife.

In fact Ryton did not keep his promise, and on 1 March Nettles and another sergeant, Thomas Elks, came to the house of the butcher John Gyttens to take Ryton away into custody. This may not seem very generous on Nettles' part, but he had little option if he was not to pay the debt himself, a sum equivalent to about one or two month's income for a master craftsman. But Ryton's wife was bitter, calling him a *'false villain'*, an accusation which provoked Nettles to sue her in the Small Court for defamation. Such events give an insight into a society rich in personal connections, where the consequences of a simple lawsuit could affect many.

Lower Castle Gate

Prison

Ryton's case shows that prisoners could sometimes be kept under house arrest. Otherwise they were taken to the gaols in their respective wards at the Stone, Welsh and Castle Gates. The latter had an upper and lower section - hence the present street name, Castle Gates. The lower or outer gate was flanked with round towers and bore the figure (now on the south side of the Market Hall) of an angel holding the arms of France and England. It did not, however, contain the prison which was located in the upper or 'Burgess' Gate. This ancient structure abutted the site where the grammar school was built, and in August 1580 its inner side was graced with the town and royal arms - perhaps replacing those of Edward IV painted in silver in 1464. It was used not only for the town's prisoners but also

Upper Castle Gate

sometimes for those of the county, although the borough council tried to prevent this in 1578.

On the Welsh Bridge the main gate, which probably contained the prison, was built upon the pier nearest Mardol. Its tower was one of the most impressive structures in Shrewsbury. Beneath the medieval battlements facing Frankwell was a niche containing the statue of a knight in armour, re-erected on the Market Hall after the old bridge was demolished in the 1790s.
Recent investigations have convincingly argued that it represents the Black Prince. This is confirmed by a reference in the murage accounts in 1463-4 to a payment for painting the likeness of the *'prince'* on the Welsh Gate in crimson and verdigris (green copper pigment). The Mardol side of the tower was rebuilt in Tudor times, probably in 1576-7, and decorated with columns and other motifs in the new classical style, together with the town arms and the cross of St. George.

The Welsh Bridge

At the same time a tenement was erected on the Frankwell end of the bridge with a line of shops perched over the water (see illustration).

One of these shops, belonging to a shoemaker, was badly damaged by fire in October 1601 after a candle had been left alight. The Frankwell end was also guarded by an outer gate comprising a squat tower and a wooden drawbridge, renewed in 1574-5.

On the other side of town the Stone Gate prison was also kept within a great tower, standing on the fifth pier of the bridge from the town side. Above the arch, facing the town, were the arms of the Earl of Shrewsbury, the crest of the Prince of Wales, and the town arms. The royal arms were also displayed, probably on the other side of the tower, carved upon the back of a sculptural stone which may have been removed after the Reformation from St. Winifred's shrine in the abbey.
Entry to the town at the west end of the bridge seems, to judge from the Burghley map, to have been through another smaller archway. Much of the Stone Gate was brought down during

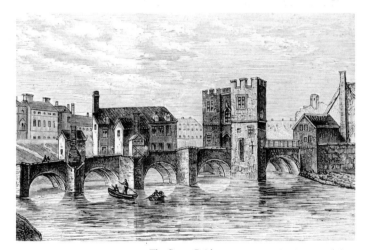

The Stone Bridge

a great flood in the morning of 23 January 1546, but was rebuilt by the end of 1552 *'in better force and comelier fashion than before'*. A drawbridge, repaired in 1583-4, connected the gate to a small island, from where the Monks' bridge arched across a branch of the Rea brook and some once marshy ground, known as Merivale, to the abbey precinct. In the late fifteenth century a bitter dispute broke out between the burgesses and the abbot over the jurisdiction of this area. The abbot complained to the courts at Westminster and had his rights upheld in 1512. As a result, if the Shrewsbury sergeants wished to pass over the drawbridge to perform their duties in Coleham, they had to hide their maces of office under their belts until they reached the middle arch of Coleham Bridge. More argument broke out later in 1527, but the burgesses had the last laugh when the abbey was dissolved in 1540 and its franchises granted to the town two years later.

Salopians involved in lawsuits could either be imprisoned in one of the gates for failing to appear in court after process had been served, or as a way of getting them to pay sums awarded against them by the court. In fact imprisonment on these grounds was less common in Tudor times than it became later because most defendants were able to find pledges or bail. The majority of prisoners were detained for failing to pay fines imposed by the Great Court or for breaches of the peace and other offences. In 1584 when the outgoing bailiffs made their annual inventory of prisoners and implements, there were 44 town prisoners in the three gaols, of whom 16 had been imprisoned as a result of legal proceedings in the Small Court, 18 for affray fines and 10 others for miscellaneous offences such as swearing, committing adultery and shooting a gun. Each prison was equipped with shackles, locks, bolts and a long iron chain used to link prisoners together. In the Castle Gate there was also a set of neck chains, while the Welsh Gate had another chain fixed to the wall of a dungeon beneath the upper prison.

It was notorious that imprisoned debtors could languish for years if they were unable to satisfy their creditors. In the 1590s the shearman Robert Higgins, complaining that he had been in gaol for almost three years, asked the bailiffs to send for his creditors and to take some *'christianlike order'*.

As he put it, *'by his imprisonment both they and he are continual losers'*. But it was not only creditors who could be uncharitable. After being gaoled for a *'small fault'* on a Saturday night (no doubt a fight), Adam Bowen requested his godfather, the town clerk Adam Mytton, to have a good word for him with the bailiffs, adding that his mother was using all her means to keep him in prison. *'She sendeth me neither fire nor candles'*, he went on, *'nor anything to sustain my body, and unless godfather you find a means presently to get me discharged, I am like here to perish'*.

Bowen's plight shows how prison could be used to stiffen discipline within the household. Everyone knew how bad conditions could be. John Edwards, lying in the Welsh Gate in 1624, even petitioned for his release on the grounds that he was a diseased cripple emitting *'an unwholesome smell'*.

A gaoler

As he pointed out, in the previous year a poor man from Pulley gaoled in the Stone Gate had spread sickness among the other inmates. An equally worrying aspect of prison, as Bowen's letter also shows, was getting enough sustenance to survive. No public provision existed, so prisoners had to rely upon their own families and friends to bring food or money to pay the gaoler for 'garnish'. Lonely and destitute prisoners had to rely on charitable donations. About 1620 the prisoner Margaret English complained that she was unable to get to the prison door to beg for relief, and was *'like to perish for want of food'*.

Relieving chained prisoners (from a stained glass window)

She asked if the door could be kept open during the day so that *'good and well disposed people'* could actually see her. *'Although they set irons upon me'*, she added, *'I shall be contented'*. Edward Flowell also once complained that since he was chained up with the county prisoners, they grabbed their share of any doles that came his way, even though he was a prisoner of the town's. To prevent this injustice, he asked to

be locked onto the town chain instead. Flowell was probably a suspected felon, committed for a serious crime. By contrast, imprisoned debtors or their pledges, as the Ryton case illustrates, had more freedom. In the 1590s, for instance, they were allowed out of the Castle Gate to purchase meat and bacon from the butchers and prepare their own meals at the house of the shearman Edward Petton.

Gaol breaks were attempted from time to time, as in 1588 when suspected felons in the Burgess Gate unfastened their bolts and chains on a January night and began to pull away the stone on the school side. They were obviously incarcerated in the dank room in the west tower which is known to have lain partly below street level. The breach was therefore too far below the ground and the sound of their labours also gave them away. When the gaoler arrived from his quarters, he found desperate prisoners with iron bolts in their hands, ready to brain the first men who came in through the door. Armed men were then called in, and order restored. For one previous felon at least, liberation was quite unplanned. When the Stone Gate came crashing down during the flood in January 1546, the prisoner was left suspended over the surging torrent, still shackled to the floor. Miraculously he survived, and was later given a free pardon for this sign of God's providence.

Prynce of Abbey Foregate

If the parties in a lawsuit got as far as pleading their case, they would nearly always employ an attorney. The basic fee for an attorney at this date was quite cheap: in 1559 it was set at 8d for cases above £2, and 4d below. Most of the Shrewsbury attorneys were craftsmen, often from the leather trades, who did legal work to supplement their income. In the early sixteenth century two or three attorneys were sufficient to deal with most of the business in the Small Court, but with the increase in litigation after 1550 the number rose, and competition to be admitted an attorney became fierce. By the late 1570s about ten attorneys were practising in the court, a figure which the attorneys themselves complained was too high. Numbers had increased faster than the growth of litigation, and there was not enough business to go around. In 1582 the borough council agreed to lower the number to eight, and in 1586 it was reduced further to six. By 1600, the most active attorney John Biston could earn a respectable £20-30 a year from fees, preparing pleadings, and attending trials.

Originally pleading had been done orally in court. But by the sixteenth century, the pleadings were drawn up on paper and, after exchange between the attorneys, they were filed in the town clerk's office. Different kinds of action had to be pleaded in different ways, and there were numerous technical slips which an attorney had to avoid, otherwise the case would be lost. A bit of book learning would have helped, but most of the Shrewsbury attorneys probably picked up their knowledge from other practitioners.

In medieval times people had a simple, rough idea of what a wrong was and how it should be corrected, and the Law was seen as the practical procedure used to bring that about. But in Tudor times there was a great change in thinking, and the Law came to be seen much more as it is today - as a body of learning which can tell us what is lawful or not in any particular case. As a result of this and other changes, pleadings became increasingly complex and learned after 1550. Shrewsbury attorneys began to make more mistakes, and were often obliged to re-draft their pleadings. To do this it was necessary to get advice from a 'counsellor' (barrister) for a fee of five shillings. Counsellors were also frequently employed to draft arguments on points of law known as demurrers. Among those who did this kind of work in Elizabethan Shrewsbury were John Brooke of Madeley Court; Thomas Medlicott, Queen's Solicitor at the Council in the Marches; Roger Pope who lived on the site of the dissolved Austin Friars; and Richard Barker of Norton near Wroxeter, twice MP for Shrewsbury, who became a judge and later the borough's recorder. But without a doubt the most interesting of such men was Richard Prynce.

Prynce's Place, 'Whitehall'

Today Prynce is best known for the red sandstone mansion, called much later 'Whitehall', which he built among the fields on the edge of the Abbey Foregate between 1578 and 1582 using stones from the abbey, although the interior walls are timber-framed. The building is important as being among the first known double-pile country houses in England, and it certainly impressed contemporaries - a *'famous house'* as one described it. Undoubtedly the litigation boom was one reason why some lawyers like Prynce and Judge Owen of Condover Hall were able to earn enough money to undertake such ambitious buildings. So too was the confused state of the land law; landowners were desperate to secure legal certainty for their property, and the services of a talented lawyer such as Prynce who knew the ins and outs of conveyancing were eagerly sought. These advantages, allied with hard work, eventually earned him a fortune.

Prynce was probably descended from a farming family from Castle Pulverbatch, although his father had set up as a shoemaker in Shrewsbury, residing in Dogpole until the late 1520s when he moved across the river to the Abbey Foregate, later becoming warden of the hospital of St. Giles. Richard himself began his career as a clerk working for the attorney John Aylesbury, and took on his first case in the Small Court in 1547. He practised there intermittently until 1551, but his ambitions were higher. In April 1554 he was specially admitted to the Inner Temple in London to study law. The special admission was probably due to his age: most students at the Inns of Court entered in their late teens, but Prynce must have been in his thirties, and was probably already practising as a counsellor before the Council in the Marches at Ludlow. Later he was elected MP for Ludlow in 1558 and Bridgnorth in 1559, in both cases probably through Council connections. But Prynce was never called to the bar. In April 1560 he was elected town clerk of Shrewsbury and gave up his rooms in London. He was sworn on 16 August but served only briefly, resigning by 1562.

With the huge profits from his career Prynce was able to amass extensive properties in Shropshire and Montgomeryshire, calculated some years after his death in 1598 to have been worth about £850 a year in rents. Despite his humble origins, Prynce used his fortune to set up his family in the first rank of the county gentry, marrying into the Leighton family of Plaish Hall, and taking out a grant of arms in 1584. Much of his inheritance was dissipated after Prynce's death by his son Francis, a boorish drone, but it was rebuilt by his second son, also called Richard, who was appointed sheriff of Shropshire in 1627 and knighted in 1632. A memorial to Sir Richard, recording his success in rebuilding the family property, exists in the abbey church.

Prynce, however, was not only a great provincial counsellor: he also has a small but not insignificant place in the history of the legal profession. Until the second half of the sixteenth century there was no explicit rule that a counsellor had first to be called to the bar before he could practise. So long as he was recognized to be learned in the law, the lack of this qualification as an 'utter-barrister' did not necessarily matter. This was true of Prynce who returned to Shrewsbury on a permanent basis

without ever being called to the bar. From the 1540s, however, the legal profession increasingly came to feel that this qualification was essential for a counsellor. In the 1570s Prynce himself seems to have been temporarily displaced from the court at Ludlow, but in 1577 he was restored by order of the Privy Council itself. Later in 1586, in recognition of his long service before the Council in the Marches, this special licence to continue in practice was confirmed. Then in 1589 Prynce became involved in a quarrel with another Shropshire lawyer called Richard Broughton who sued him in one of the central law courts at Westminster. In the course of the action Prynce's professional qualifications were again called in question. Although the lawsuit was probably never decided, 'Prynce's case', as it became known, effectively established that in future no counsellor could practise before the superior law courts who had not first been called to the bar of one of the Inns of Court in London.

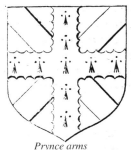

Prynce arms

Juries and wager of law

The object of pleading was to narrow the dispute between the plaintiff and the defendant down to one point known as the issue, which could then be submitted either to wager of law or to jury trial. In the sixteenth century about ten to fifteen per cent of all cases entered in the court books were eventually tested by one or other type of proof. Wager of law was only permitted in certain kinds of actions, mainly involving debts arising from informal oral agreements - for example, to pay a craftsman for weaving some cloth. The method of proof was very simple. Having got to the issue by denying the plaintiff's claim and asking to wage his or her law, a defendant had to produce by the next court day a set number of compurgators or 'hands' to swear on oath that the defendant's denial was true. If the hands managed to do that without a slip, the plaintiff was 'in mercy' and lost the case.

In the early sixteenth century Shrewsbury defendants were normally asked to find two hands, although sometimes more were required, especially if the defendant was an outsider or was thought to be untrustworthy.

On the face of it wager of law might seem to have been an open invitation to perjury. In fact it worked better than one might suppose, and about forty per cent of all defendants who attempted to wage their law failed to do so. That was because in a small community, where people's dealings were known to many, few would risk their reputation by swearing on behalf of a defendant who was thought to be lying. All the same, defendants did have less chance of success if the case was tried instead by a jury, and after 1540 wager of law fell out of favour. But it did not become extinct until much later, the last case where it was allowed occurring in 1683.

If defendants did not wish to wage their law, or it was not permitted, they had to put themselves 'on the country', in other words ask for a jury trial. It was also possible for a jury to sit if defendants had allowed an action for damages to go against them by default, in which case an inquest for damages as it was known, would have to decide how large the damages should be. Today jury trial in non-criminal cases is only allowed in libel, but in Tudor times civil juries of this kind dealt with many different types of lawsuit. Jury service was common and was one of the most important ways in which ordinary craftsmen took part in the running of their towns. In Shrewsbury the three sergeants were normally responsible for drawing up lists of potential jurors in their wards, from which the twelve men were sworn. If not enough men turned up to be sworn, the court could select people who happened to be standing about nearby, known as *'tales'* men, until the full number of twelve had been secured. Making up the juries was a sensitive job, and they were sometimes challenged because a sergeant was said to be connected to either the plaintiff or the defendant. About 158 a genealogical diagram was sent to the court showing that the defendant John Byston and the sergeant Richard ap Richard

were descended from the same great-great-grandfather (see illustration). In such cases two impartial individuals called 'leasors' could be selected to choose the jury instead.

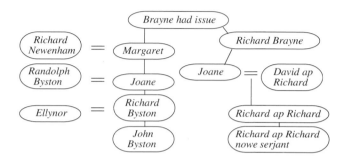

Apart from inquests for damages, there were two kinds of juries in civil cases. A common jury would hear a whole group of cases, whereas a special jury, paid for by the litigants, would hear only one. Trials themselves were held in the Guildhall on selected jury days; there were 27 such days in the civic year 1587-8 for example. Parties could employ a counsellor and produce witnesses, but not give evidence on their own behalf. From October 1574 the jurymen were able to retire to the room at the lower end of the Guildhall to consider their verdicts, although a jury chamber is also mentioned earlier in 1523. In most cases tried by a common jury proceedings were pretty rapid and verdicts were arrived at within a few minutes. But in complex cases in which a lot was at stake, usually involving land, the jurymen could take much longer. This could be a problem because juries were not permitted food or drink once they had retired. On Tuesday 30 July 1594 a special jury went into the jury room at 6 o'clock in the evening. At 8 p.m. on Thursday they were still there unable to agree, and the situation was getting desperate. The bailiffs then persuaded the litigants to take their dispute to arbitration; *'and so upon the same'*, as a contemporary described, *'the jury came out as aforesaid, weak enough, especially some of them, if they had tarried one night longer had* [would have] *died'*.

Chapter 7 - **Making a Living**

Trades, streets and housing

It is impossible to describe here all the different livelihoods in Tudor Shrewsbury, some of which, like leather-working, had changed little since medieval times (see Dorothy Cromarty, *Everyday Life in Medieval Shrewsbury*). Instead a few can be selected to evoke different aspects of work and its environment. In 1520 a town of Shrewsbury's size would have had about sixty different occupations, most of them servicing its own needs and those of its market region. It is true that many clothworkers worked for a wider market because of the Welsh cloth trade, but their importance in the economy should not be exaggerated. Even in periods when the cloth trade was booming, the whole textile sector, including the weavers, comprised less than one third of all masters in the town. The leather workers in particular were almost as numerous. As trade increased after 1560, and some groups in society prospered, new occupations and specializations also sprang up to satisfy demand, such as upholsterers, silk weavers (by 1576 - they produced ribbons on narrow looms) and watchmakers (by 1634). Stationers and booksellers too appear for the first time in their own right. In the 1580s the London printer and publisher Roger Ward kept a shop in Shrewsbury containing over five hundred titles, most of them popular devotional manuals and grammar school texts. Perhaps it was in a shop such as this that the schoolmaster John Baker purchased the fifteen books on arithmetic and geography which he left to the school library in 1608, together with 23 little maps and two maps of the world, *'one in two circles and one in straight lines'*.

The distribution of trades in Shrewsbury was very typical of towns in this period. Because of water requirements and the stink from their works, the dyers tended to congregate away from the centre near the river, particularly in Frankwell, for centuries the main area for the trade. For the same reason, some of the most

Houses in Bridge Street, opposite Romaldesham Hall

important tanneries were located in Romaldesham (Barker Street and Bridge Street). In the sixteenth century the most successful of the tanners living here were the Montgomerys, one of whom, Thomas Montgomery, was elected bailiff in 1545, 1556 and 1560. The family resided in Romaldesham Hall on the west side of the present Bridge Street.

The house was a large timber-framed building entered by a porch which projected six feet into the street. Inside, the hall floor was laid with two huge figures, seven feet long in blue and white cement, representing Gog and Magog. In the arch above the fireplace were three stones carved with the town arms and the arms and crest of the Montgomerys. When the building was demolished about 1760, the stones were re-used in the frontages of the terraced houses built upon the site, and could still be seen there until those houses too were knocked down in 1949.

Chimney stones from Romaldesham Hall

The suburbs also saw distinct concentrations of labourers, especially in the Castle Foregate. Of the 21 male householders residing there in 1525, six were building workers in the Carpenters' company and at least ten others were wage-earners 'out of craft' who would have earned their living by casual labour, such as scouring ditches and laying cobble stones. There were other concentrations of tradesmen in Shrewsbury, some of which became more pronounced after 1560, although the potters who had gathered in Coleham by 1300 (Dorothy Cromarty, *Everyday Life in Medieval Shrewsbury*, pp. 11, 57-8) had disappeared by 1500. In general, however, these concentrations were less notable than the intermingling of trades. In 1525, for example, some 34 corvisors (shoemakers) headed households in Shrewsbury, of whom eleven lived in Corvisors

Shoemaker's shop

Row (Pride Hill), seven of them virtually adjacent to each other. Although this comprised the greatest density of shoemakers in the town, most corvisors nonetheless lived elsewhere. Conversely most of the other 30 male householders in Corvisors Row had other occupations. They included four tailors, three shearmen, three butchers, two barbers, two cappers, a doctor, a mercer, a bowyer and a cooper. Some of them had very modest businesses, as tax records of the same date show. Yet living among their number that year was Adam Mytton, a leading member of the town gentry, who was to serve as bailiff on seven occasions and was elected one of the town's two MPs in 1523, 1529,

Mytton arms

1536 and 1542. He also became a member of the Council in the Marches, served as sheriff for both Shropshire and Radnorshire and was knighted in 1547. Mytton's case was a typical example of the way in which prominent citizens, even though they tended to reside in the principal streets in the town, still lived in close proximity to humble craftsmen.

Depending on the site, townsfolk by the beginning of our period could be housed in different ways. One solution, appropriate for a narrow burgage plot, was to build at right angles to the street, with a shop on the ground floor, a chamber or 'solar' above, and an open hall and service room behind, stretching backwards down the plot. A likely example once existed at 8A Castle Street. Before it was demolished to make way for Littlewood's, the blackened timbers in the fine crown-post roof of the hall, caused by smoke curling up from the open hearth, could still be seen. Alternatively, if the site was less cramped, perhaps because two plots were run together, the house could be built front-on to the street. The open hall could then lie immediately behind (e.g. 1-2 Fish Street), or be placed with the solar on a jettied floor above the shop, although sometimes a second floor was also added (e.g. 'Henry Tudor' house on Wyle Cop). Access to the upper rooms could be had either by an internal ladder or stair, or from the backyard. Another option for wealthy burgesses was to invest in a row of shops along the street frontage; a passage then led to a courtyard at the back, alongside which ran the hall and other chambers. In the Middle Ages, the grandest of these halls had been built of stone, and an interesting group of them, of which Bennett's Hall was one (see Chapter 3), had been sited on the north side of Pride Hill.

Developers could also build additional floors above the shops for living accommodation, creating a block of tenements. Ireland's Mansion and the earlier Abbot's House in Butcher Row are good examples, although the architectural details differ. The latter was a commercial development by Lilleshall abbey which owned much property around Fish Street. Recent ring dating indicates that the timbers were cut down about 1457;

The Abbot's House

and this fits an item in the bailiffs' accounts which shows that the *'Abbot's House'* there was completed in 1459 when a special reward was given to the carpenters, while the abbot himself was fêted with wine on the same day. The shop fronts on the ground floor are a rare survival. Customers did not usually enter the shop but made their purchases over a sill or a board which could be raised and tied up with rope to form a shutter. Cutting these window ropes was a favourite prank of alehouse drunks. In the 1530s a tenement on a prime site like the Abbot's House could be rented for between ten and twenty shillings a year (more by the seventeenth century after inflation), although tenants might only live there, renting a shop elsewhere. By contrast, the single-roomed cottages of the poor, run up in terraces or along a shut, could be had for much less than five shillings a year.

Documentary evidence from other places suggests that as the population rose in the century after 1550 and the shortage of space became more acute, houses tended to grow in height, especially in the centre of towns. One late house of this period, depicted in 1858, stood in Mardol and was six storeys high,

Six storey house in Mardol

Plaster ceiling at 127 Frankwell

including the garrets. At the same time, open halls where they existed began to disappear. Once they had provided access to other rooms, and been used for cooking and eating; but in time floors or ceilings were inserted, and halls were often turned into specialized kitchens, with eating and general living taking place in the increasingly comfortable surroundings of the parlour. The insertion of a chimney and a ceiling in the Council Chamber in 1578 reflects the kind of changes that were occurring in existing domestic houses at the same time. New Elizabethan houses, like Perche's Mansion or 127 Frankwell, could reflect fashions immediately. Both contain a large room on the first floor with a ceiling of moulded plaster - the successor in effect to the medieval first-floor open hall.

Wool and cloth

In the Middle Ages Shrewsbury had provided some of the greatest wool merchants in England, exporting fine Shropshire wools to Flanders. The trade still existed in the fifteenth century, now channelled through the great market or 'staple' at Calais. Shrewsbury merchants continued to play an active role, like Alderman Thomas Stone, who lent money to the Crown for the defence of Calais in 1450, and Thomas Ottley, once

Plaster ceiling at Perche's Mansion

mayor of the staple, who purchased the estate at Pitchford before his death in 1486. The scale of the trade is illustrated by a contract made in June 1497 by another prominent Shrewsbury merchant, William Sugdon, who had served as bailiff in 1479: he agreed to supply 21 sacks of march wool weighing 577 stones to a merchant of the Calais staple for £221 - although it was later claimed that when the wool was delivered, it proved to be of inadequate quality and weight. The Calais connection explains why the Crown sometimes used Shrewsbury men as agents to provision the garrison there. The stapler John Bayly was employed in this way in the 1510s. He was issued with letters of protection giving him free passage and security from arrest. Between 1516 and 1519 he used these letters on three occasions to block lawsuits brought against him in the Small Court.

In time this international trade in wool declined in importance. This was due to a great shift in the economy away from the export of raw wool to the export of cloths made in England. But this change simply meant that the merchants could now service a home market instead, since Shropshire wools were popular with the broadcloth manufacturers of Worcester city, Gloucestershire and Somerset. In 1584, for instance, 200 'tods' of wool (about 400 stone) were sold in Shrewsbury to a clothier from Shepton Mallet, to be shipped via Bristol. By the 1560s superior march wools were also sought by the cloth-making towns of Essex such as Coggeshall and Dedham. The Shrewsbury stapler George Leigh was active in this trade. Each year about June clothiers came up from the south to sample the wool in his warehouse. After selection the wool was then forwarded at the end of August to the Maiden Head inn at St. Giles-within-the-fields in Middlesex.

Leigh was a major figure in Shrewsbury, elected as one of the town's two MPs on six occasions, and as bailiff in 1564, 1568 and 1574. He lived in Dogpole, and was chosen by the Lord President of the Council in the Marches, Sir Henry Sidney, to take his son Philip into his household as a boarder in 1564 after Philip's admission to Shrewsbury school. Two years later

Philip stood godfather to Leigh's son, who was named after him. Like other staplers, Leigh employed agents to travel around farms in the region looking for supplies. In 1565, for example, his servants negotiated a contract with the sheep farmer Matthew Jaxson of Llanymynech to supply a half or full stone of wool each Michaelmas until 1567. After the summer shearing, clips were delivered to Leigh's warehouse - identified perhaps by a merchant's mark like that which survives on an external window jamb at Pride Hill Chambers, now a McDonald's restaurant. Fleeces of slaughtered sheep could also be processed in buildings like the Fellmongers' Hall in Frankwell (c. 1570) which still survives, complete with the central entrance for carts coming in from the countryside. Wool processing and tanning were still operating there as recently as the 1970s.

Merchant's mark at Pride Hill Chambers

Fellmongers' Hall

the rear entrance to the back yard before later alteration - a sight that must have been familiar to generations of Salopian carriers as they loaded up their animals before setting off towards London or the villages in the south west of the county.

Unicorn Inn, 1877

Shrewsbury wool merchants were invariably members of the Drapers' company, better known for its connection with the Welsh cloth trade. The basic organization of this trade in Tudor times is well known, with the merchants purchasing the cloth from the farmer-weavers at Oswestry and Welshpool, having it sheared in Shrewsbury, and then sending it down by carrier to the Thursday market in Blackwell Hall in London. Complaints about the carriers were common. A typical case was that of Hugh Beynes in 1557 who sued the carrier Richard Arrowsmith for failing to carry a pack of cloth down to London in time for the market, with the result that Beynes *'hath run into displeasure with his customers'*. In 1730 the carriage of goods to London was still done by pack-horses, most of them setting off from the 'Pheasant' in Under the Wyle - no doubt the Lion and Pheasant which still exists. Across the road lay the Unicorn, another well-known carriers' inn, part of which is now occupied by Tanners wine merchants. Although the Unicorn is known to have been in existence by 1719, its earlier history is still obscure. Architectural evidence, however, indicates that the original building was rebuilt about 1603. A lithograph of 1877 shows

By the 1550s the normal practice was to sell cloth taken up to London to wholesalers who might ship it abroad, although at least one Shrewsbury merchant, Roger Knyght (five times bailiff between 1465 and 1488), is known earlier to have attended the great cloth market at Antwerp in person, lending money to other merchants there, repayable in London by means of a 'bill of exchange'. It would be a mistake, however, to concentrate only upon the Welsh cloth trade. Shrewsbury merchants dealt in a very wide range of cloths for the local market. When the draper Thomas Hanley died about 1550, for example, his shop was stocked with over 360 yards of cloth, including northern 'marble', Welsh 'russet' and Irish 'fledge'. The northern cloths were coloured red and orange, but Shrewsbury drapers are also known to have purchased undyed 'kendals' from chapmen coming down with their pack horses from the north-west and the Lake District. These were narrow cloths, woven from poor quality wools, and used for outer garments or light summer coats.

The variety of cloths stocked by the drapers is also illustrated by a purchase about 1505 by a Wem customer. As well as kendals, the sale included worsteds (using yarn spun from long fibre wools) and kerseys, which were thick cloths woven in twill order, napped and then shorn on the back. Kerseys were suitable for warm but comfortable garments like stockings. The draper stocked two varieties, one from Lichfield and the other from Monmouth. In addition there were cottons, friezes and rugs, which were cloths suitable for linings and coarser garments, as well as two types of linen and 1 1/2 yard of fustian - probably a velvet imported from Europe. A skilful and experienced draper would have an intimate knowledge of these and many other types of cloth and linen, of how much they were worth and what markets there were for each.

Friezing, cottoning and shearing

Strictly speaking Welsh cloths were so named after the origin of the wools used in their manufacture, and in this sense cloths of this kind were also made by weavers in Shrewsbury. But whether they were made in town, or brought in by the merchants from the border markets, the cloths were then washed and stretched-dried on frames called tenters, sited at different locations including Frankwell. In 1532 a tenter belonging to the merchant Roger Wylkes was hired out to the shearman Roger Browne for 7s 6d. The cloth was then raised to a fluffy nap by scuffing the surface with a hand-held staff set with the bristly heads of the teasel plant. Court cases show that in the 1560s a teasel staff could be bought for between 2s 6d and 4s, while 1,000 teasels were purchased by the shearman John ap Gwyllym in 1566 for 6s. Over 4,000 teasels were also listed in a shearman's inventory in 1589. Clothworkers obviously got through them at a fast rate, and for this reason they were tempted to use a wooden block set with metal wires called a card or rubber. Although cards lasted much longer than teasels,

Raising the nap (from a 15th century stained glass window)

they were disliked by the drapers because they damaged the fabric. Parts of Somerset (near the Cheddar Gorge) and perhaps Gloucestershire too, specialized in the teasel crop, and Shrewsbury probably imported them up the Severn. Certainly court cases show that teasel staffs were brought up river by bargemen from Bewdley and Tewkesbury.

With the type of cloth known as a frieze the nap on one side was raised into tufted beads by a circular scrubbing motion. The nap was left uncropped and made up the inside of hardwearing winter garments, doublets and jerkins. By contrast, the nap of a 'cotton' cloth was cropped closely by the shearman to leave a uniform and

At the shearing board

even surface. Cottons were normally made from narrow cloths, and were suitable for petticoats, waistcoats, cloak and coat linings. Cloth for shearing was placed upon a board and cropped using huge shears, the shape of which remained much the same for centuries before the introduction of mechanization in the nineteenth century. The handle was supported by one hand, while the other worked the upper blade. In 1574 and 1585 the Shearmen's company raised money for a grindle stone to sharpen the blades, although grinding itself was a skilled task done by travelling craftsmen.

Because it became a finishing centre for Welsh cloths, Shrewsbury had one of the highest densities of shearmen in the country, many of them congregating by the seventeenth century in Shoplatch and Murivance (Swan Hill). Still working largely in domestic workshops, they were notoriously dependent upon the drapers for providing them with work, and numerous disputes occurred over piece rates and slow payment. Not every merchant behaved like the draper John Mynton who died in 1550 and was said to have been *'a true occupier and dealed justly with all those shearmen that wrought for him. He never stopped with them any penny but paid them always ready money'*.

Cappers and fullers

At the end of the fifteenth century caps became very fashionable in England, and in Shrewsbury, as in other West Midland towns, there was a mini boom in capmaking. Some seventeen cappers headed their own households by 1525 - at least double the number in 1480. By 1522 the trade was sufficiently numerous for its journeymen, and presumably its masters too, to be allotted a place in the Corpus Christi procession. Most of these masters were in the parent Mercers' company, but a few were 'out of craft' and resisted admission to that fellowship. John Asprey, for example, had worked for fifteen years as a capper outside the company before the Mercers sought to shut up the windows of his shop, and appealed successfully to the Council in the Marches to force him to pay his entry fine.

Water carrier with flat cap

Asprey's stubbornness is understandable: cappers were among the poorest artisans in town, and the size of their admission fees to the parent company was inappropriate to their income. The Council in the Marches seems to have recognized this, and with Asprey's admission the fees for cappers were reduced.

Caps, which could be sold for about 2s, were made in much the same way as berets are today. The cap was first knitted and then beaten in water in the fulling mill to shrink it to size.

In 1521 the capper Thomas Barbur delivered 24 blue caps and 36 white caps to David Walker for fulling, although Walker was later said to have destroyed them in the mill. The services of the fullers, of course, were also required by the weavers, and many lawsuits in the town court involved allegations of faulty workmanship by the fullers. In July 1562, for instance, the weaver Roger Wyllyams delivered 11 yards of white kersey straight from the loom to Thomas Bartelemew to full within the next fortnight, but at least half of the cloth was later destroyed. Court records show that many cloths were in fact fulled in the countryside, especially at Leebotwood. Fullers from that village appear in Shrewsbury records throughout the Tudor period. When two of the villagers were bound over to keep the peace in Shrewsbury in 1534, their pledges included three weavers and one capper, indicating the kind of personal and trading connections that existed.

After about 1550 caps fell out of fashion, to be replaced by broad-rimmed felted hats, like those worn by the barge hauliers depicted on the Burghley map. Cappers from many towns complained about the decay of trade, and parliament passed a law in 1570-1 requiring most people to wear a cap on Sundays and holidays. Several Salopians, including the curate of St. Mary's, are known to have been fined in 1574 for wearing hats and not caps on the Sabbath, but the dictates of fashion proved too strong, and caps disappeared from the people's heads.

Victuals and dearth

June 1577 was a month of buffeting winds and torrential rain as, one after another, low pressure systems swept across the country. Since the annual harvest was so crucial to life, there was great anxiety that the price of bread corn would begin to rise, a sense of vulnerability reflected by the many observations on the weather made by the town's chronicler. Four years earlier he noted that the winter had been so dry and cold that many cattle had died for lack of fodder, and the price of rye and wheat had both risen. The blossom had not come out until the end of May, and there was a late harvest over much of the country. The dependence of towns upon the harvest and a regular provision of food and drink meant that the authorities were obliged to supervise the victuallers with the greatest care. Traditionally this was done by regulating prices and supply by means of an 'assize'. Shrewsbury streeters kept up continual pressure to ensure that the bailiffs kept the assize and that victuals were available at fair prices: *'look to it for the love of God'*, as the Shoplatch streeters instructed in 1548. In 1569 the bailiffs themselves were presented by the Mardol streeters, *'because ye will not look to the weighing of bread according to old custom'*.

Particular anxiety was expressed after a poor harvest, as in 1551 when the bailiffs were asked to regulate the butchers, bakers and brewers, *'or else the poor people are not able to live'*. Unusually large numbers of people were also presented for engrossing

the market - that is purchasing in bulk to re-sell at a profit. Next year the streeters of Corvisors Row complained that Bailiff Roger Pope himself had bought up 20 or 30 bushels of rye and sold it on to some Welsh customers. This kind of deal was regarded as especially immoral since it denied townsfolk the chance to buy corn in their own market. *'What respect of conscience is in him or regard of others'*, as the streeters put it.

Bull and bear-baiting

Even in normal years there was a steady trickle of presentments for abuses by the victuallers. Butchers in particular were often accused of making their meat look more attractive by blowing up the flesh with air - an old trick. In 1592 the butcher Thomas Jones was also presented for killing a bull without first baiting it - necessary because baiting was thought to tenderize the meat. A bull ring used for the purpose was located close to Coleham Bridge.

The burgesses could also exercise some control over the meat market through their ownership of the fleshboards in Butcher Row (then part of Fish Street). Eleven of these boards had been rebuilt in 1468, and by 1580 they were rented out for 7s a year. Despite their location, it was only later that the butchers began to live in Fish Street in large numbers. In 1525, only two of the sixteen male householders residing there came from that trade. By 1668, however, 21 out of the 46 male householders were butchers, and there were others around the corner on Pride Hill. As the butcher Richard Stubb once explained to the bailiffs, it was a custom that the meat stalls *'should always descend and come to the use of the nearest and next of kin, being butcher, of any tenant which should use the same'*. This reflected the fact that butchering tended to run in families. Examples in Tudor Shrewsbury included the Dawes, Botfield, Stubb, Clarke and Gittyns families. Lawsuits show that such men rented local pastures in which to graze their animals - Bicton, Nesscliffe and Welbatch are places mentioned - and like the leather workers who also kept their own flocks, they participated in a small way in the wool trade.

When in March 1536 the butchers were suspected of trying to raise prices by boycotting the market, a survey found that five of the butchers had 222 wethers, 50 sheep, 16 oxen and two pigs out at pasture. The borough council threatened to throw the market open to victuallers from the countryside if the butchers did not amend their ways. This was a traditional means of countering such abuses. It was employed in the same year against the bakers who had deliberately stopped producing

a cheap kind of rye loaf known as housewife's bread. On another occasion, however, about the 1570s, it was the bailiffs who ordered a temporary stop to the baking of fine and penny cakes, apparently because there was then a shortage of dairy produce, although the wardens of the Bakers' company later proposed that fine cakes could still be made if customers brought their own butter. The Bakers' company in fact was often in dispute with the corporation, particularly over a much resented lump sum paid since the 1490s by the company in place of a toll known as Sergeants' Fee. Suspicion of the town's victuallers was by no means unfounded. In 1534 the butchers themselves admitted a plan to stop slaughtering, and similar conspiracies were also discovered in other years. Problems of this kind also occurred with the production of tallow candles which was largely controlled by the butchers, and many orders were made over the years to ensure adequate supplies.

Corn prices in Shrewsbury are known to have been dangerously high after bad or disastrous harvests in 1527, 1550, 1556, 1586, 1594-5, and 1596-7. The last two failures in particular came close to catastrophe. By the winter of 1597 the price of rye had reached 12s a bushel and wheat between 14s and 15s - about four times higher than normal - rising even further by May. Unusually large numbers of people were buried in the town's parishes during the year, not necessarily due to starvation but to secondary illnesses caused by malnutrition. Drastic steps were needed and London agents were contracted to import 3,200 bushels of grain from Denmark and Danzig (Gdansk in Poland), which was then shipped up river from Bristol and sold at two thirds the going price. There were desperate scenes in the market as the poor clamoured for the cheap penny loaves specially baked to relieve them.

Similar measures had been taken in 1586, and were again in the winter of 1598 when grain was obtained from Norfolk and the continent. In the meantime the bailiffs patrolled the Cornmarket urging farmers to charge a reasonable price. After criticizing Mrs. Wood, a farmer's wife from Alberbury, in February for the price of her corn, she bluntly told them that it was none of their business. When her servant also shouted out that his mistress hadn't come to town to buy wit or borrow wisdom, he was immediately arrested and thrown into prison. Bad feeling was now abroad, and the Woods later brought a lawsuit against the corporation for extorting illegal tolls, witness to the bitter tensions which could arise between town and country in years of dearth.

It is obvious from such evidence that bread, especially rye bread, was the basic fare of Shrewsbury's poor, eaten perhaps with a bit of cheese. Meat was a rare item in their diet, although the price of pork set in May 1536 during a shortage of victuals at a half penny a pound, and mutton and veal at a little more, would have been within reach of a labourer's family if the father was in work. Butchers' stocks suggest that mutton was the most commonly available meat, although some families also kept their own pigs. In 1544-5 there were 69 of these animals in town, kept by 54 individuals; by 1618-19 numbers had grown to at least 160 pigs and 95 owners. It is clear all the same that only a minority of the population could rely on their own supplies of pork and bacon in dearth years. Otherwise people would have to turn to butchers like Richard Davies who had at least twelve pigs rooting around the gardens of Coleham in 1618, much to the disgust of the streeters there. Vagrant pigs could only be kept within the walls on payment of a fine, and all had to be yoked or ringed, a necessary precaution as the case of Robert Swayne in 1589 illustrates. He was presented at the Great Court and subsequently fined after his sow had bitten and seriously injured some children playing in the street.

In 1587 the writer William Harrison noted that vegetables had also become an important part of the English diet, and not only among the poor. Sixteen years later, however, the Shrewsbury dyer Richard Gardiner (see chapter 4) claimed that Shropshire had yet to appreciate the benefits of market gardening. It was a fault he was determined to remedy before he died, and in 1603 he published his *Profitable Instructions For The*

Manuring, Sowing and Planting of Kitchen Gardens, based on a lifetime of horticultural practice. Some of his techniques would startle a gardener today - such as steeping cucumber seeds overnight in fresh milk before planting. But other comments still strike a chord, including his observation on the Cabbage White: *'those caterpillars do never repent until they come to Tyburn or the gallows'*. (London criminals were hanged at Tyburn, now Marble Arch.) Above all, Gardiner wanted to show how valuable vegetables could be to the poor. With just four acres planted, he had been able during the great dearth to relieve hundreds of poor people in the pinching weeks before the harvest. *'And many of the poor said to me they had nothing to eat but only carrots and cabbages which they had of me for many days, and but only water to drink. They had commonly six wax pounds of small close cabbages for a penny to the poor. And in this manner I did serve them, and they were wonderful glad to have them, most humbly praising God for them'.* Gardiner's sensitivity was not unusual among the rich since food shortages posed a real threat to public order. After the harvest failed in 1585, for example, there were fierce protests by the Mardol streeters that rye was being shipped downstream by barge *'to our utter destruction'*; and in June the following year a *'great tumult'* broke out at the High Cross after some of the bakers had refused to accept the assize of bread.

'First-brewed Shrewsbury ale'

At the beginning of the fifteenth century 'first-brewed Shrewsbury ale', as the Welsh bard Iolo Goch described it, was sold in Wales and border towns like Oswestry, indicating that some drink at least must have been sold wholesale. This is supported by a claim in 1417 that the Shrewsbury draper John Schetton had brewed and sold 480 gallons of ale each week while serving as bailiff. But most brewing at that date was still small-scale, carried out by alesellers or 'bribsters' on their own premises. Lists of these bribsters were kept by the town authorities, and they show that in the fifteenth century the great majority of them were women and housewives, often brewing

Bribster woman

it was thought to adulterate the drink. Several brewers, for example, were presented in 1536-7 for using hops, and as late as 1549 the Mardol streeters presented the brewers *'because of hops, ashes and other trumpery withall'*.

In the 1520s the biggest brewer in Shrewsbury was John Davies, a member of the Drapers' company. He lived in Mardol, which with Knockyn Street was the area most closely linked to the trade. His tax assessment in 1524-5 was one of the highest in the town, indicating his prosperity. Many years later in May 1556 he sold out to another draper, disposing of a lead brewing furnace; a malt mill with its stones; a bay gelding to draw it; and a pipe to convey water to the furnace from the Severn. Davies was obviously one of the emerging wholesale or 'common' brewers who came to dominate the trade. Another is known to have set up in business in the Abbey Foregate in 1580, but the most famous in later years was William Rowley, elected bailiff in 1628, whose brick mansion in Knockyn Street, built in 1618, still survives in much altered form. (His grand-daughter married John Hill, related to the Hills of Hawkestone and mayor in 1688-9, after whom the street is now named.) In 1635 Rowley was said to have *'a vast brewhouse* [Rowley's House] ...

and selling for only part of the year. In theory they were listed and fined only if they broke the assize of ale, but in practice all bribsters were normally included, although burgesses were omitted for a time in the sixteenth century. The system in fact was a kind of informal licensing.

In the Tudor period female bribsters were largely replaced by men. This change occurred all over the country, and one cause is thought to have been the introduction of hops. Originally ale had been brewed from fermented grain only, usually barley. The result was often a bland, rather muddy drink, although herbs were sometimes included to improve the taste. Adding hops produced a clearer brew, or 'beer' in its strict sense. The new process was technically more complicated, and because beer also lasted longer than ale, it encouraged bigger individual brewings. In the long run these developments helped to squeeze women and other small brewers out of the trade. All the same, hopping was at first banned in Shrewsbury in 1519 because

Rowley's Mansion

the brewing vessels wherein are capable of 100 measures', and some of his customers, and those of other brewers, are recorded in 1621-2, buying at 12s a barrel.

This trend towards wholesaling received official support in 1601 when the bailiffs appointed official brewers to serve the town and tried to suppress the 'pan-brewers' of the alehouses, although innkeepers were allowed to brew if they wished. Traditionally each alehouse with drink on tap advertised itself by hanging out a pole or stake with a bush on the end, although painted signs had begun to appear by 1600. Signmakers are known to have been working in Shrewsbury by 1632 at least.

Alehouse with sign

This change too is thought to reflect the appearance of more permanent establishments, now buying in their drink rather than brewing it occasionally themselves. Prices were regulated by the assize and checked by ale-tasters (mentioned in 1522 and 1553). Officially four pints could be bought for ld in 1553, three pints in 1584 and two pints in 1592 (but four pints still for a 'second' beer or ale).

In the 1560s there were about sixty alesellers in Shrewsbury (excluding the Abbey Foregate), little more than there had been a century before. By 1625 there were more than 160, scattered all over town, run mainly by lowly craftsmen and poor widows. Although the number of alehouses per head in Shrewsbury changed little (about one for every 45 inhabitants), the increase in numbers was regarded by the authorities with alarm, and in 1592 the sergeants were instructed to list all the householders selling ale or beer, with a view to suppressing *'the great number of alehouses being one of the great fears of this Commonwealth'*. This anxiety was part of a growing panic on the part of respectable society as the population grew and economic pressures mounted. Alehouses were seen as nests of criminality and idleness, subverting the discipline of the household, while puritans hated them as dens of vice. In theory their numbers could be controlled by using the licensing powers given to JPs by statute in 1495 and 1552. Licensing was operating in Shrewsbury by 1568, but regulation was very difficult to enforce, and the number of all alesellers continued to be much higher than those who actually obtained licences from the JPs. Even William Rowley, who was one of the leading puritans in Shrewsbury, is known to have sold beer to unlicensed alesellers.

In fact alehouses played a valuable role in the precarious lives of humble craftsmen and the urban poor. Often they were places where money could be borrowed, simple lodgings found and some warmth obtained. Even respectable Salopians might prefer to take their custom to an alehouse run by a cherished landlady rather than the more expensive taverns which sold wine (three of which had been allowed by an Act in 1553). When Widow Hamlet, said to be ninety years of age, was presented in 1632 for unlicensed aleselling, John Meighen and the other masters of the grammar school sent in a testimonial on her behalf, stating that during term-time she served a most valuable function. Food too could be purchased at the alehouse. In 1576 the apprentice Richard Wildinge who was accused of spending his master's money in the alehouses, had been able to buy cakes, custard, woodcock pies and other meats.

In this respect alehouses now served the same function as
the cook shops of earlier centuries (see Dorothy Cromarty,
Life in Medieval Shrewsbury, p. 41). The cooks themselves had
once had their own company with a place in the Corpus Christi
procession, but by Tudor times they had been absorbed in other
companies. Perhaps the greatest cook, in effect a chef, in
Elizabethan Shrewsbury was John Hassold, a member of the
Glovers' company. He is known to have cooked for the Leighton
family at Plaish Hall in 1582, and it was his establishment that
the Shearmen's company patronized in 1584 before going
to Kingsland to practise archery (see chapter 4). It was not,
however, a male but a female cook who prepared the feast for
the tax commissioners meeting in town in September 1598.
As well as bread and beer, the meal included stewed broth,
capon and mutton; powdered beef and cabbage; three geese;
a pig; roast beef; four rabbits; 14 pigeons; two custards;
four pear pies; venison baked in flour; and fruit and cheese.
Guests did not eat a whole course as such, but took a bit from
each treat provided. Their pleasure was far removed from the
experience of the poor who were still recovering from the
miseries of the great dearth.

Carpentry and brick

Several Shrewsbury houses built after 1550 display a distinctive
style, including the use of cable-moulded pilasters ending in
grotesque heads, sunken quatrefoils, diagonal struts, and tie
beams and barge boards carved with vine trails. Examples which
no longer exist included Lloyd's Mansion in the Cornmarket
(1570) and Merivale House (1601) beside the former Court
House of the Abbey Foregate. Some of the motifs of the
Shrewsbury style hark back to the screenwork of late medieval
churches, particularly in the Welsh Marches where many
Shrewsbury carpenters are known to have come from.
Craftsmen in allied trades may have had similar geographical
connections. The Welsh painter John ap Atha who lived in
High Pavement and whose clients in the early sixteenth century
included the churchwardens of Felton parish near Oswestry,

Merivale House, 1601

Gable on Lloyd's Mansion

is known to have once worked with Jevan ap Dakkyn of Llanbrynmair in Montgomeryshire.

The Shrewsbury style can also be identified at Pitchford Hall, Penkridge Hall (Leebotwood), Netley Old Hall and Albright Hussey, showing that Shrewsbury carpenters also found work in the countryside. In 1517, for example, the carpenter Thomas Forsbroke who lived in the Stone Ward, contracted to build a frame for the churchwardens of Cound parish which was also an important site for quarries supplying heavy roofing slates. These Harnage slates, as they were known, were used on several Shrewsbury buildings, including Lloyd's Mansion, the earliest known example of the Shrewsbury style within the town itself. Shropshire slates were also obtained from Corndon hill, although the 13,000 slates purchased by the churchwardens of St. Mary's in 1580 after a great storm, and shipped up-river from Bristol, had probably come from the great slate quarries in Cornwall. Local clay tiles were also used, and lawsuits in the 1520s and 1560s show that Old Heath and Derfald just north of town (east of the Ellesmere road) were places where tiles and bricks were manufactured. By 1478 tilers had also begun to dig for sand under Coton Hill. Of about 18 building workers who owed appearance at the Great Court in 1525, seven can be identified as tilers or 'shinglers' of whom five were living in the Castle Foregate, close to the brick fields. Orders of 1523 and 1577 show that their trade was strictly demarcated: tile and brickmakers could not become layers, and vice versa. Brick was probably used mainly for chimney stacks, like that in the King's Head pub, Mardol, on which a painting of about 1450 to 1520 was discovered in 1987. In 1507 John Gosenell agreed to make a chimney eight foot wide of brick-lime and sand for the skinner Lewis Baugh of Knockyn Street for 13s 4d and the re-furring of his old gown.

Tiles and bricks had an obvious safety advantage over timber and thatch which were prone to catch fire. The chronicler recorded ten fires in Shrewsbury between 1575 and 1601, often started by unattended candles and malt kilns or the storage of damp hay.

The authorities were well aware of the dangers: only the bakers, for example, who needed fuel for their ovens, were permitted to store gorse (which was collected from the heaths just north of town) and faggots within the walls. But thatching at least was not prohibited until the new by-laws of 1638, although this measure proved difficult to enforce. Residents were still being presented for using thatch in the 1710s, even in important streets like Wyle Cop and Romaldesham.

Timber too remained the principal building material throughout the Tudor period, and for many years afterwards. Even chimneys could be constructed of wood, although this practice was also banned in 1638. The use of brick to build a whole house, as in Rowley's Mansion of 1618, was exceptional, although the brickman William Corwyn of Castle Foregate

Lloyd's Mansion and the Market Hall in 1859

is known to have made a substantial contract in 1557 to build a brick chimney of four fireplaces and supply 24,000 bricks for a John Gough of The Marsh. Corwyn was also involved in building the brick privy for Lloyd's Mansion in 1573 - a more modest but probably more typical job. His wife obviously found his bricks a handy weapon against her neighbours. In August 1556 she threw one at Margery Mylton, cracking her on the knee. Margery then sued for damages in the Small Court, moaning that she was now crippled *'to the utter undoing of this plaintiff for ever in this world'*.

Carpenters' marks (drawn by H. E. Forrest)

Buildings constructed in a box-frame of pegged timbers were very adaptable: old timbers could be replaced and new bays added on with relative ease. A good example was the agreement made between the weaver Humphrey Leaton and the carpenter John ap Rees in December 1590. Leaton already had an old frame of two bays, but wanted ap Rees to restore it by inserting joists, tie-beams, purlins and rafters, adding on a third bay with a portal, door and transom window. According to ap Rees a payment of 33s 6d had been agreed, but when he came to inspect the old frame he found that many more timbers were missing than he had been led to believe. The contract was re-negotiated, and ap Rees began working *'with speed and in good sort, as far forth as such crooked and warped timber would suffer him'*. This was a reference to the old timbers that ap Rees recycled for the renovation. Seasoned oak was too hard to cut easily with existing tools, so carpenters worked with fresh wood which tended to distort after being set in the frame. New timbers were prepared beforehand, and marked at the ends with Roman numerals and other signs to indicate the position in which each timber should be inserted. A good run of these marks can be seen on the side of the former Liberal Club on the corner of Milk Street (Belmont) and Spicers Lane (Belmont Bank), and others exist on buildings in Grope Lane.

Trows and float waters

The Burghley map shows a trow being hauled upstream towards the Stone Bridge by four bargemen, using a rope attached to the mast. No doubt it was by this method that two Bewdley men had transported unspecified goods, probably grain, from Bristol to Shrewsbury in 1537, receiving five shillings as a reward from the bailiffs. By the 1620s two or three of these trows, with a carrying capacity of twenty tons or less, are known to have run a fairly regular service between Shrewsbury and Bristol throughout the year. They had a very shallow draught and no keel, travelling downstream on the current, or raising sails if the wind was in the right quarter. In the estuary boards were let over the sides to serve as temporary keels. Lawsuits and port records show that cargoes going downstream from Shrewsbury included wool, cloth, ale, dairy products, honey, skins and leather. Upstream came wine, alum (for fixing dyes and tawing skins), pig-iron from the Forest of Dean, teasel staffs, coal from the Broseley area, and malt. Later on tobacco and luxury groceries were also imported in substantial quantities.

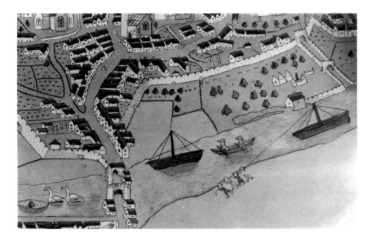

In 1618 it was said that the river bank beside the Grey Friars was a favourite site for unloading barges and other boats. By contrast, the water by the postern gate at Bulgerlode just upstream from the Stone Bridge was too shallow, although this problem was later rectified by building a wharf there. When the river was in spate, however, the bargemen often secured their vessels by throwing lines over the walls of the old Dominican friary at the bottom of St. Mary Waterlode. They then had a right of way to the Stone Bridge along a strip of land or 'stang' (shown on the Burghley map), which separated the Severn from an old backwater. For the brewers and merchants living across town, loading and unloading was made much easier by the construction in 1606 of Mardol quay on the south-east side of the Welsh Bridge. The waterfront was 44 yards long, and the project was undertaken by the mercer Rowland Jenks who rented the site from the corporation, taking tolls in return. One shilling

was paid for a barge-load of coal or timber, while 4d a ton (2d for burgesses) was charged for all other goods.

Another aspect of the river trade is also depicted on the Burghley map - the transport of timber by means of rafts or 'float woods'. Many references to this trade occur in lawsuits in the Small

Court, especially during the sixteenth century. Timbers were lashed together at places such as Alberbury and floated down the Severn whenever there was a good run or 'float water'. Wood was in great demand by the dyers, tanners and brewers for their furnaces, and it is not surprising that they were sometimes presented for engrossing the market. In 1534, for example, Thomas Cherwell (another brewer who lived in Knockyn Street) was accused of buying up floats for 4d a yard and selling them on for 8d. But Cherwell is also known in 1532 to have kept stocks of coal. Like Richard Hollyns of Acton Reynald who purchased a cart-load of coal from Oakengates in July 1561, he presumably obtained his supplies from the east Shropshire coalfield. There are other references to carts of coal coming to Shrewsbury in the early sixteenth century, indicating that over short distances at least the cost of transporting coal by road was still competitive at that date.

There were several fish weirs on the Severn in Shropshire, including one at Coton, built in 1448, which was managed by the town. Barges could avoid them by using cuttings, but floats had more difficulty. About 1520, for example, six Welsh floatmen petitioned for redress after £3 worth of wood coming to town on the last float water had got stuck in the weirs. Problems of this kind were common in the early sixteenth century, and tenants of weirs in the liberties (e.g. at Montford in 1506 and Mytton in 1531) were presented or prosecuted in the courts. A Commission for Sewers, with powers to keep inland waterways open, began work around Shrewsbury in 1525 and again later in 1575. A more natural hazard appeared in 1564 after the county had been lashed for eleven days by ferocious storms: two oak trees near Berwick were uprooted and slid upright into the Severn. They remained in that position for many weeks, obstructing the passage of floats down the river, before eventually being pulled aside.

Later in 1586 and 1593 the mercer George Trevenant was also presented for impounding the river above the Stone Bridge and erecting fish traps under his house there. Bargemen from Mardol complained that passage was obstructed, and that the safety of one of the arches was threatened. The traps were obviously associated with the mill on the bridge which Trevenant's father had rented from the corporation for 10s a year in 1565. Many of the river workers and floatmen were Welsh who began to congregate in the streets around the Welsh Bridge. Complaints about weirs nearly always came from the Mardol streeters. When we find that at least 13 of the 21 male householders living in Knockyn Street in 1563 were Welshmen with the patronymic 'ap' ('son of'), we can guess that the concentration of river workers in that quarter was already well advanced. By 1668 Frankwell, Mardol and Knockyn Street had 23 trowmen, 10 watermen, 3 hauliers and 2 shipwrights. Floats may have been obstructed by weirs but they posed their own dangers too. In March 1579 a float smacked into a prop on the Stone Bridge supporting some old shops, which then collapsed into the Severn. A butcher's child, aged four, was carried down in the crash, but by a miracle was saved. It was because of incidents like this that shooting floats through the bridges had been banned in 1536. Seven years later eight residents, including the dyer John Gardiner and the tanner Thomas Montgomery, were fined for floating 99 yards of wood through the arches. The potential perils were well illustrated by the fate of the three Clarke brothers in January 1599. They were carrying a load of timber downstream in their barge and tried to shoot the Welsh Bridge; but the bow struck one of the arches and turned their vessel sideways on to the stream, pitching them into the water. Only one of them survived.

Gambling Dick

Beyond the world of work Salopian men at least enjoyed a rich variety of recreations. These included bowling, bear and bull-baiting, hare-coursing, wild-fowling, and hunting (tradesmen are known to have gone poaching for rabbit and deer in Ercall park with crossbows). Patrons of the Gullet tavern in Shoplatch could also play real tennis at the court enclosed there within a wall, although a stable had been built over the court by 1630. Numerous references in the records show that townsfolk were also entertained by professional musicians, actors, animal-keepers and acrobats, travelling from town to town. For example, the play put on in the Guildhall by The Lady Elizabeth's Men in 1613 on the night of the great Exchequer robbery, was attended by craftsmen, servants and the daughter of at least one master. For the boys, of course, there was always football. The complaint of Widow Susan Jones about 1620 was probably not untypical. According to her account, six lads had played so much football and *'cat and dog'* in the castle grounds that the grass had been trodden bare. (She was tenant of the castle which had been ruinous since at least the 1530s, and had been granted to the town by royal charter in 1586.) Another pastime popular with young men, as we saw in chapter 2, was fencing with wasters or swords. In the 1620s the barber Richard Gough was a skilled practitioner: he hung his foils up at work and gave lessons in a room above a joiner's shop. Among those who came to him for instruction was Alexander Gyttyns from Worthen, moaning that he *'did somewhat despair in his own judgement of the science of defence'*.

The gentry also enjoyed the pleasures of hawking. The Langleys are known to have gone hawking for partridges in fields near the Abbey Foregate. A trained bird of course was a valuable asset: in November 1558 in Dogpole the gentleman Edward Onslow sold a goshawk to Gilbert Astley, Esq., for the sum of £5 6s 8d - equivalent to a year's income for a poor craftsman. A major stimulus for gentry recreations was gambling. A case in point was the wager on a horse race between Peter Langley and Francis Prynce (son of Richard)

Hawking

in September 1613, to start at the Hattons' house in the Abbey Foregate. Each was allowed one other rider, but Francis turned up at the off with his two brothers and three servants, leading to accusations of cheating and an unseemly slanging match. We can guess that on such occasions other inhabitants would also have taken the chance to lay bets among themselves. That was certainly the case at the great cockfight during the Easter holidays in 1597, attended by lords, knights and other gentry. On one side were the cocks of Cheshire and Lancashire; on the other, the cocks of Shropshire and Wales, supported by birds brought up from London. The cockpit was set up in the backyard of the gaoler Richard Horton, and the Shearmen's

company provided warders to control the crowds. Prodigious sums of money were won and lost, victory in the end going to the cocks of the north.

Gambling was also closely linked to the sport of archery. In February 1571, for example, the miller John Madder lost 10s to Griffith Waltore of Rowton in a contest at Meole Brace. The winner promised a return match for the same stake, giving Madder odds of five arrows to four in a contest of rovers.

By this date, however, archery was declining rapidly as the use of firearms became more common. This development took place all over Europe, and is illustrated by the inventories of arms taken at the Shrewsbury musters. In December 1569 the companies possessed just 12 arquebuses, calivers (a type of musket) and hand-guns, compared to 81 calivers and 20 muskets in 1587. The number of sets of bows and arrows remained about the same at 80 in 1569 and 75 in 1587 which, given the growth of population, represented a proportional decline in ownership. Gunpowder makers also began to work in town, like Christopher Russell whose goods in 1575 included a brass furnace, square *'coffins'* for keeping potassium nitrate, 23 tubs, 1 1/2 pound of gunpowder, and a grinding mill. Not surprisingly there were complaints from the bow and arrow makers about the neglect of long-bow practice: archery butts were being taken down and craftsmen were playing bowls instead at houses like 'The Hermitage' on the Longden road, once the residence of the Spelcross hermit (see chapter 9), but now it seems an alehouse.

Perhaps the most popular recreation of all, however, was dicing whose perils were illustrated by the fate of the credulous Richard Bibbye. On a Saturday in May 1586 he was enticed by John Poyner into playing a game of dice in Frankwell. They went first to the house of the weaver Richard Tidder where Bibbye lost 3s 4d. At night they met again, and he lost 10s more. On Sunday Bibbye borrowed 20s and returned to Tidder's house where Poyner and two other craftsmen were playing. He lost that too. Next day Bibbye obtained another 20s. Some of it had already been gambled away before he appeared at Poyner's own house, taking the precaution this time to mark the dice. But his luck was no better until he discovered that Poyner had swapped the dice under the table. He left in a rage, going over to the house of George Phelips, and there lost all. On Tuesday Bibbye sold 17s worth of malt and rushed back to Phelips's table. Poyner was also there, but Bibbye was undeterred. Soon all this money too had gone. Next Saturday he squandered another 19s lld, and offered in vain to pawn some cloth for 20s more. In seven days he had lost well over £4. At that rate a modest craftsman would have been destroyed by debt within weeks. It was because of such dangers, and the fear that gaming would distract craftsmen from archery practice, that Parliament had long sought to restrain it by statute. In this case Poyner himself was privately presented and later fined for unlawful gaming. But the pleasures of gambling, then as ever, proved too great to suppress.

Noethrift

Noethrift's a gamester that with cardes and dice
mastes whats his oune, yet's full of Auarice
Of rounds he mackes noe small account he dare
Hazard his soule vpon a dye thats square,

'Noethrift', the dicer

Chapter 8 - Crime and the Common Peace

Felonies and misdemeanours

Long before Tudor times English law distinguished two kinds
of crime. On the one hand there were serious wrongs called
felonies, punishable in theory by death and confiscation of lands
and personal goods. On the other there were lesser wrongs or
'misdemeanours', which could lead to imprisonment, corporal
punishment or a fine. As we have already seen, many
misdemeanours in Shrewsbury were dealt with by the Great
Court, but some, such as assault, were also handled by the
Shrewsbury sessions, the court at which most felonies were
prosecuted. Except perhaps for murder, which was difficult to
conceal, it is impossible to discover the real levels of felonious
crime. The records only tell us which felonies were most likely
to end up before the courts.

Of these, by far the most common in Shrewsbury, as elsewhere,
were crimes against property, such as burglary, pick-pocketing
and larceny (theft). Some thieves were semi-professionals,
like the cut-purses who are known to have pestered the Abbey
Foregate fairs in 1589 and 1593, but many acted simply on the
spur of the moment. A typical example was that of the Essex
man passing through town in 1592 who had gone drinking in
an alehouse in the Abbey Foregate. After walking out into the
field at the back to relieve himself, he found a smock lying
at the bottom of a fence post on which it had probably been
hung up to dry. He picked it up and later sold it for eight pence.
Another example involved John Smith, the haberdasher who
had come to town to watch the Whitsun play in 1569.
While the spectators were making their way back home from

Cut-purse

the dry quarry after the performance, Smith took up a hat that
had been left behind and carried it back to his lodgings in the

89

house of the tanner George Higgons. There he removed a gold brooch pinned to the hat and pawned the brooch next day for 10 shillings. It was probably this action that gave him away, as the loss of the hat had already been proclaimed throughout the town. Smith was then questioned by the bailiffs and bound over to appear before them at 20 days notice. In another case in February 1579 the shearman William Eakine was accused of stealing a hatchet belonging to the carpenter Roger Smyth who was working on a frame near St. John's Hill. At first Eakine said that his son had borrowed it to do some chopping at home; but later he admitted taking the hatchet to pawn it and get a few pence to buy some victuals, *'being in great need thereof'*.

Most criminal prosecutions for larceny involved opportunist thefts of this kind, although there is some evidence for more organized crime. In December 157 a gang holed up overnight in a barn near Shelton intending to rob the drapers next day as they rode to Oswestry market. But the word got out, precautions were taken and *'the thieves having intelligence shrunk away'*. In 1591 another band of thirty to forty men was said to be roaming the countryside near Shrewsbury. Merchants riding to Oswestry had been attacked and some £2,000 was alleged to have been stolen. The Deputy Lieutenant and the JPs of the county assembled at Easter at Shrewsbury to take counter-measures, and the town bailiffs were instructed to keep strict watch and ward. Next year on the night of 27 November an attempt was also made to burgle Richard Prynce's mansion in the Abbey Foregate by breaking into his counting house. Although only a small amount of money was found, the keys to the rest of the house were also kept there. That gave the thieves an opportunity to search the other rooms, but they were disturbed by a sudden noise and fled. Unfortunately for them, when they got outside they found that their horses had slipped their tethers. It was too dark to see where the animals had gone so they had to leg it instead. Next morning two saddled horses were found wandering in the fields, and these were brought into town to see if anyone could recognize them. A more successful crime (initially at least) was the great Exchequer robbery in 1613

when six thieves took advantage of the distraction caused by the performance of a play in the Guildhall to break into the Exchequer and make off with the huge sum of almost £230 belonging to the town stock.

Since there was no police force, detection of a felony had to be done by the victim or the community at large. The constables or sergeants were normally employed only to arrest suspects and to transport them to the bailiffs for questioning. Detection techniques were simple, such as noting odd behaviour or the appearance of stolen goods in someone else's possession. In 1564 Gwen Chapman was lying in bed on a Sunday morning when Joan Phillips, a glover's wife, came in and asked her to keep a bag full of gloves. Later in the afternoon Joan returned with some more gloves. Shortly afterwards Gwen learnt that a glover's shop had been broken into, so she reported Joan's behaviour to the common sergeant. Joan's husband was then questioned by the bailiffs and imprisoned on suspicion of felony. In the case of the Exchequer robbery, the criminals virtually gave themselves away by going on a reckless gambling spree in the county. The miller William Dennys, for instance, was observed *'prodigally wasting his money'* at dice, cards and cockfighting at Halesowen.

Other felons were craftier. In August 1551 an old woman called Elizabeth Bickerstaff was murdered in St. Chad's parish by Thomas Bickerstaff and an accomplice. The crime was a particularly wicked one since Thomas was a kinsman whom Elizabeth had brought up from an early age. Her body was then chopped up and buried in the bare ground beneath her bed. Next day Thomas went out feigning distress, asking that a search be made for her in case she had got lost or drowned. Nothing of course was found until seven weeks later when the landlord came round to collect some unpaid rents. When his dog began to scrape beneath the bed suspicions were immediately aroused. The ground was dug up and Elizabeth's dismembered body was found, mixed up with sheep heads and other bones.

Occasionally a victim or a constable might still raise the ancient 'hue and cry', verbally summoning all adult males to apprehend a felon. On a Saturday in January 1596, for example, an Oswestry gentleman called Thomas Evans was run through the body with a rapier during a street brawl beside the Red Lion on the Wyle Cop. His killer, a trumpeter called Richard Twisse, immediately mounted a horse and galloped furiously through the town. He had no time to risk crossing the Welsh Bridge, but splashed frantically across the river instead. In the confusion it was some time before it was realized that Evans was dead. The hue and cry was raised, but by then Twisse had gone. Another successful escape was also made by Thomas Davys, one of the bailiffs' sergeants, about 1541. He had killed a journeyman shoemaker on the Welsh Bridge, but immediately fled as far as Calais, later receiving a pardon.

By that date it was no longer possible for murderers and other felons to claim the old privilege of common sanctuary in a church since it had been effectively abolished by statutes in 1530 and 1540. But felons are known to have sought sanctuary before then in the Austin Friars in 1472, 1477 and 1525, and in St. Chad's in 1493. The full privilege of common sanctuary lasted only 40 days. After that it was an offence to feed the felon, so it was advisable to put the church under guard to prevent his escape and so starve him out or force him to abjure the realm. When two felons sought refuge in the Austin Friars in 1477, for example, carpenters were employed to build a special enclosure to shut them in. If the felon elected to abjure the realm, he had to confess his crime before one of the coroners and was then assigned a port from which to depart into exile. The full procedure was the same as it had been in the 1300s, as Dorothy Cromarty has described (*Everyday Life in Medieval Shrewsbury*, p. 89).

In cases of felony there were two principal options open to the victim once a suspect had been identified. The first was to notify the bailiffs that a private criminal prosecution, known as the appeal of felony, would be brought at the next sessions. The second option was to bring the suspect before the bailiffs to see if they thought that there was sufficient evidence to begin a public prosecution. In their role as Justices of the Peace the bailiffs would then question the parties and witnesses on oath, assess the evidence and the characters of those involved, and then decide whether proceedings should continue. If so, suspects were either bound over to appear at the next sessions or sent in the meantime to prison. This system of examination had been formally set up by statute in the 1550s. After that date the town clerk, acting as clerk of the peace, attended the bailiffs, either in the Exchequer or in their private studies at home, and jotted down the statements on paper. The bailiffs also had summary powers at this stage to punish other petty offenders brought before them such as swearers and vagrants, by sending them for a short time to the stocks, the Cornmarket pillory, gaol, or (from the 1630s) to the House of Correction.

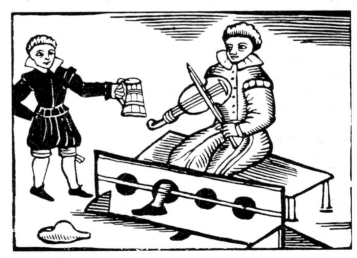

In the stocks

A typical case was that of the labourer Thomas Smyth who in October 1537 was placed in the pillory after stealing 4d from the poor box in High Pavement. If possible, the bailiffs would try to arbitrate between victim and accused. Perhaps an old widow had been abusive or stolen a little piece of cloth, but she was poor and had not given trouble before. Wouldn't it be better to be charitable and forgive her? In such ways the bailiffs sought to reconcile the parties and restore the common peace of the community.

Assizes and sessions

If no reconciliation was possible, or the alleged offence was too serious, the accused would have to be prosecuted at the sessions, although victims of petty theft could alternatively sue for damages in the Small Court. Shrewsbury had been granted the right to hold its own sessions in 1445; before then town criminals had been dealt with at the Shropshire sessions. Serious felonies could also be tried at the assizes, although in Tudor times Shrewsbury handled most cases of this kind itself. Twice a year in Lent and Summer two judges from the central law courts came round on circuit to try criminal and civil cases in the county. Until the late sixteenth century these assizes were often held at Bridgnorth or sometimes Ludlow, but in 1579, after a long interval, sittings were resumed at Shrewsbury where eventually, in the eighteenth century, they were permanently fixed.

The assizes were major social occasions for the county gentry. The judges were escorted into town by the sheriff who was also expected to lay on a great show of hospitality.

In August 1599 the sheriff Sir Edward Kynaston of Oteley near Ellesmere *'kept open house to all comers for beer and beef and sumptuous cheer at his set table for gentlemen strangers and men of account'*. On the same occasion the town found lodgings, wood and charcoal for the visitors and their 'trains' of servants

Arms of Kynaston of Oteley

and followers, while 15 beds were also provided by the craft fellowships. Fine cakes, sugar, barrels of beer and wine were purchased for provisions, and rushes and flowers were also used to decorate the judges' seats.

If the weather was fine, the assizes were held not in the Guildhall but in the open air, as in 1591 when a seat for the Lord Chief Baron was erected outside in the street. The entrance to two shops was blocked off and both craftsmen were compensated for their loss of trade. Later on, a temporary court room was usually erected for the purpose beneath the new Market Hall. We can get some idea of the excitement caused by the coming of the assizes from an incident in 1603. On 16 March several people were leaning out of a window to catch a glimpse of the judges as they came out of the hall where they were dining when a rotten sill suddenly gave way beneath them and crashed on top of an apprentice who was holding the judges' horses. He was badly injured and his life imperilled.

Like the assizes, the Shropshire sessions were also usually held in Shrewsbury by 1600. In theory these courts were held four times a year at Epiphany, Easter, Trinity and Michaelmas - hence the use of the term 'Quarter Sessions' to describe them. But the town's own sessions did not always have enough business to sit so regularly, especially in the first half of the sixteenth century before the growth of the population. On the other hand, it was possible to convene a special sessions at other times of the year to deal with riots and trespasses - the case of the Shearmen's tree in 1591 and the occupation of the school in 1608 were both examples.

If victims of a felony decided to bring a private criminal prosecution by appeal of felony, the case was handled in the same way as a civil lawsuit. For various reasons this was quite a tricky process, and although the appeal was a common form of prosecution before 1550, afterwards it began to fall out of use. The records suggest that appeals were often brought simply to annoy neighbours without intent to take the case as far as trial.

In 1509 Thomas Powys brought an appeal against the butcher Hugh ap John, but failed to appear at the sessions to prosecute his suit. As practice required, proclamation was then made three times in court that if anyone else wanted to prosecute ap John for the alleged felony while he was still standing at the bar, they should come forward. No-one did, so the butcher was then released, and Powys was fined 6s 8d for failing to appear.

Increasingly, the more normal method to prosecute a felony was by an 'indictment' in the King's name. An indictment was an accusation made by twelve or more jurymen sworn to inquire on the King's behalf. In practice, draft indictments were drawn up beforehand in the town clerk's office using the evidence already obtained by the bailiffs during their questioning of suspects. These drafts were written out on 'bills' and then submitted to the so-called Grand Jury for consideration, in much the same way as misdemeanours were written out on the streeters' bills and submitted to the Great Inquest.

In the pillory

The Grand Jury's job was not to try suspected felons and lesser offenders, but to find by majority whether an indictment was true and the King had a case against the suspect which could go forward to trial. Where a body had been discovered, a coroner's inquest of at least twelve men could also meet and state whether death had been caused by a named person, and this finding too worked just like a true indictment. In addition Grand Juries had a duty to consider presentments for other offences such as unlicensed aleselling, false weights and measures, illegal encroachments and failure to maintain the public highways. The bailiffs could then take measures to rectify the abuses. Administrative orders could also be issued concerning such problems as vagrancy, wage rates and bastardy. Later in the seventeenth century monthly sessions were also held, dealing mainly with the provision of poor relief.

Trial and the gallows

As the Grand Jury sifted through the indictment bills in the jury room, other craftsmen who had been called up for jury service would be waiting to see if they would be sworn onto the actual trial or 'Petty' Jury. The social status of these petty jurors was lower than that of the grand jurors. When Richard Fernes was indicted for sedition in 1591, for example, the Grand Jury of fifteen men included a gentleman and six drapers, among whom was Richard Chirwell, later elected bailiff in 1597. By contrast the Petty Jury comprised three bakers, three glovers, a shoemaker, a tailor, a shearman, a tanner, a weaver and a farmer.

Selecting petty jurors was the task of the coroners, and like the choice of trial juries in the Small Court could be a sensitive matter. After Hugh ap Rees and William Morris had been arrested for the murder of Chirwell's servant in 1594, a weaver's servant called Roger Wootton was chatting about the trial with the shearman David ap Thomas. Leaning over the back of the shop where Wootton was working, ap Thomas told him that Chirwell had got the coroners to pack the jury with his friends and neighbours. Despite Wootton's scepticism, he remained convinced that the jury had been rigged. In fact, Petty Juries could sometimes be too independent for the magistrates' liking. On at least two occasions in 1596 and 1609 Petty Juries are known to have been imprisoned for bringing in verdicts of not guilty, much to the disgust of the bailiffs and their steward (a prominent local lawyer or gentleman employed to give legal advice on criminal matters). In such cases, the jurors could be fined and forced to make a grovelling apology.

If the Grand Jury found bills of indictment to be true, the defendants were brought to the bar in the Guildhall and asked how they wished to plead. If the answer was 'not guilty', they were entitled to have any irons or shackles removed during their trial. The Petty Jury was then sworn in, standing face to face with the defendants who were allowed to reject up to twenty jurors in capital cases where their lives were at stake. In fact challenges were rare, and trials usually proceeded at a very brisk pace. There was no rule that each defendant should have a separate jury. In Shrewsbury the Petty Jury normally tried all the cases in one batch (usually less than half a dozen), although verdicts and sentences were not given until all the cases had been heard in turn. The atmosphere was very informal. As one trial was taking place at the bar, spectators, legal officials and waiting defendants milled about in the Guildhall, gossiping among themselves. At this date prisoners indicted for felony were not permitted to employ counsel since in theory the judge was supposed to look after their interests, although this rule did not apply to appeals of felony or indictments for misdemeanours. Defendants had to tell their stories in their own words, giving the jury a means to assess character and motivation.

This was important because Petty Juries used their moral judgement about the circumstances of a case not only to acquit defendants but also, in cases of theft, to reduce the severity of the charge. If a defendant was indicted and then convicted of stealing goods worth one shilling or more, known as grand larceny, the sentence in theory was death. But the jury could side-step this terrible prospect by finding the defendant guilty, but for a smaller sum. This was known as 'finding under the value', and was a common practice. A good example involved Eleanor Hughes, indicted in 1579 for stealing a coverlet and a canvas sheet worth 2s 6d in all. Although she was found guilty, the Petty Jury reduced the sum to just beneath the value at 11 1/2d, and she was sent to the stocks instead. In this way juries could discriminate between poor persons who had stolen out of necessity, and persistent thieves who had finally pushed the patience of the community too far. Corporal punishment of some kind was the usual punishment for criminals who escaped the gallows. A prison term was not thought to be a useful corrective, and was in any case a burden upon the resources of the community.

Even after conviction for capital felony, it was open to the bailiffs and the steward to mitigate sentence by giving the condemned, provided it was a first offence, an opportunity to read out a passage from the Book of Psalms, often the first verse of Psalm 51 called the 'neck verse'. This offer was known as benefit of clergy, and if it was accomplished successfully, the felon was branded on the left thumb with 'T' for thief or 'M' for manslayer, and saved from the gallows. Illiterate criminals of course could try to learn the verse by heart, although success was not guaranteed. At the February sessions in 1579 three thieves were offered clergy, but none could recite from the book - perhaps because they were all from Wales and knew little English. Increasingly moreover the use of benefit of clergy was restricted to the lesser felonies, and in Tudor times was never available to women, although pregnant females could claim 'benefit of belly', allowing them to postpone execution until after the birth of their child - a reprieve known to have been granted in 1580 and 1594. But juries tended to be quite sympathetic towards women. In other places at least, women are known to have been less likely to be indicted and convicted of grand larceny and other serious felonies than men.

Although charged with stealing a bag of corn, the scarcity of provisions in that desperate year was taken into account, and his life was spared.

Executions were moments of great theatre which many townsfolk would attend. The condemned were given the chance to make a last speech and make their peace before God. Spectators wanted a sign that those about to die admitted that they had done wrong and now accepted their fate. In that way the life of the community was made whole again. Less acceptable were rambling speeches of self justification, like that given by the parish clerk of the Abbey Foregate awaiting execution on Kingsland in March 1582 for counterfeiting money. Still less the behaviour of the five stubborn felons condemned at the summer assizes in 1598. They would neither repent nor pray, and when the sheriff told them to confess as an example to others, they jeered that they hadn't come there to be preached at. More appropriate was the *'godly end'* made by Richard Illedge at Old Heath in 1588, which *'greatly comforted the audience'*; or that of the shoemaker David Davies in June 1600. While returning from a visit to his uncle in the countryside, Davies had met and killed the ostler of the Red Lion. Together with the tailor James Evans, he was named as the murderer by a coroner's inquest meeting at Hadnall and later condemned to die. But whereas Evans had benefit of clergy, Davies had no reprieve. Initially at the time of his arrest and imprisonment he was *'wickedly and desperately minded'*, as the chronicler described, *'but going to his execution mortified, and died godly and patiently. God be praised'*.

The Council in the Marches

The enforcement of law and order in Shrewsbury was backed up by the Council in the Marches, set up in the late fifteenth century and not finally abolished until 1689. Its jurisdiction ran throughout Wales and the border counties, and from time to time the town was able to observe the Council's power in action. In 1579 twelve pirates were escorted through Shrewsbury

If no reprieve was obtained, convicted felons were taken a day or two later to the place of execution. In Shrewsbury gallows or 'crap trees' are known to have been erected at Montford Bridge; beside the causeway at Heath Gates on Old Heath (Ditherington roundabout); at Kingsland; and between Coleham and Meole Brace. In the latter case the gallows were located in Coleham field on the edge of the open fields of Meole Brace. The site was also known as Warrow Tree hill (warrow means gallows), near the present recreation ground at the east end of Meole Rise, and clearly visible to travellers on the Hereford road below. Gallows could also be raised near the site of the crime. In February 1583, for example, the joiner John Hill was strung up for three days on the green beside the abbey mill, looking towards his house on the Stone Bridge where he had murdered his wife. Particularly wicked criminals like Thomas Bickerstaff were hanged slowly and painfully in chains on a gibbet. Even at this late stage the condemned could still be saved. In November 1580 a maid behaved with such godly resolution as she went to the gallows that the public preacher intervened and brought her home, later begging successfully for her life. Seven persons were also condemned at the summer assizes in 1597, and again one of them was brought back at the last moment from the tree.

Old Hall of the Council House

on their way from Anglesey to Ludlow for interrogation; and in 1583 the servant of Sir Henry Sidney, the Lord President of the Council, was nailed by an ear to the Cornmarket pillory for forging his master's signature. Although the Council had its main base at the castle in Ludlow, some of its officials and the counsellors practising there also lived in Shrewsbury,

Gatehouse to the Council House

Court instead. But the Council was employed occasionally to settle big political and economic disputes. In Elizabeth's reign, for example, it heard disputes about council elections, the town commons and employment relations between the cloth merchants and the shearmen.

The Council in the Marches also had an important supervisory role, badgering the bailiffs to carry out their duties with care and diligence. After Lacon's murder on Election night in 1594, for instance, the town's steward William Fowler of Harnage Grange wrote to the bailiffs on behalf of the Council, of which he was a member, requesting them to send a progress report on their investigations. Mentioning that he had not been impressed by the two previous bailiffs, who *'would neither ask nor follow any good council'*, he added *'in the meantime have care for the return of very good jurors both for the enquiry and delivery* [i.e. the Grand and Petty Juries]; *I pray you look to your weights and measures, bread, drink and all other things ... '*

For most Salopians, however, the existence of the Council was most relevant to their daily lives when it made one of its periodic visits to the town. Like the coming of the assize judges, these were important social occasions, and the companies were again expected to provide beds and furnishings for the visitors. But whereas the judges only stayed for a few days, the Council might remain in residence for a whole law term, providing excellent business for the innkeepers and other suppliers, like Roger Wood of Crowmeole who brought in two cartloads of hay in October 1562 for the Council's use. In 1599, however, the town was caught out. Expecting the Council to stay for two terms, provisions had been laid in accordingly; but it stayed for only one, arriving on 4 June and leaving on 6 July. When in residence the Lord President stayed at the Council House beside the castle, a private dwelling owned at different times by the Newton, Onslow and Owen families and rented out to the corporation for the Council's use. It was Sir William Owen of Condover Hall who in 1620 built the attractive gatehouse which still survives. Visits were always accompanied by courteous exchanges of food

like Richard Prynce and Alderman Thomas Sherer who was the Council's chief examining clerk. The Council heard not only criminal cases but civil ones as well, although in practice Salopians only rarely took personal lawsuits involving debts and trespasses to Ludlow, preferring to use their own Small between the Council and the town. In 1538 the Lord President gave a gift of venison, and the bailiffs sent two swans and 700 oysters in return. The town kept a swannery for this purpose, probably on one of the islands by the Stone Bridge. In 1575 the nest was rented out to the dyehouse owner William Weale who lived right beside the bridge in the house which later became Jones's Mansion.

The Welsh Gate

Among ordinary townsmen, however, feelings towards the Council were not always so friendly. At the curfew hour on a June Saturday in 1583 Richard Dryhurst, one of the Lord President's attendants, was taking his uncle back to his lodgings in Frankwell, and exchanged good-nights with another gentleman at the wicket gate on the Welsh Bridge. Seven or eight watchmen were standing nearby, one of whom stepped up to Dryhurst and said, *'I will make thee give us also a good night'*, and punched him in the face. The others then jumped on him and tried to drag him off to the cage for the night. (Until 1577 this lock-up had stood on the Welsh Bridge, when it was removed to the postern gate beneath the bridge at Cripplelode. There was another cage in the Stone Ward, mentioned in 1536.) According to Dryhurst, the watchmen had been *'encouraged and set on by some of the occupiers* [craftsmen] *of this town who do malign the company attending the same Council to have mischief or murder one of the company and thereby to terrify the rest'*. Naturally the watchmen gave a different account. According to them, Dryhurst had been returning from Frankwell at about 11 p.m. and was told that next time he came that way he ought to speak to them. He answered, *'I will come this way in spite of thy teeth'*, and called them a bunch of knaves. He was arrested after a struggle but refused to disclose whose *'man'* (servant) he was. But after being threatened with the cage, he said he was a gentleman lodging with the attorney John Biston, to whose house he was then escorted.

Such incidents hint at the contempt which ordinary craftsmen and the gentry toffs who travelled around with the Council could feel towards each other.

Chapter 9 - **Church and Reformation**

Purgatory, priests and the saints

At Easter 1554 the churchwardens of St. Mary's spent 4d *'for the making of the sepulchre'* and a frame on which to set it. This was the Easter sepulchre, once the focus of one of the most important religious devotions before the Reformation. On Good Friday after commemorating Christ's passion, a barefoot priest carried a crucifix and the consecrated bread or 'host' in its vessel to a sepulchre on the north side of the chancel. In some churches this sepulchre was a permanent structure set into the wall. But more normally, as in St. Mary's, it was a moveable wooden frame covered with a pall cloth, similar to the hearse used at funerals and commemorations of the dead. Both the crucifix and the host, which had been kissed by the people during the service, were wrapped in linen and solemnly interred within the sepulchre. A guard was then normally kept over it until Easter day when all the church candles were lit and the clergy processed to the sepulchre to honour it with burning frankincense, the purchase of which is also recorded in the accounts of St. Mary's churchwardens. The host was then removed to its usual position in the hanging vessel or 'pyx' above the high altar while the bells were rung and the anthem *Christus Resurgens* was sung. In the meantime the crucifix was placed on an altar on the north side, and venerated by the people creeping barefoot and on their knees to kiss the foot of the cross - a practice which also took place in a different context on Good Friday.

The Easter sepulchre dramatized the meaning of the Resurrection to the Christian believer. But it was only one of a rich variety of religious ceremonies that would once have been familiar to Salopians. Another was the practice during Lent of hanging a great veil in front of the Crucifix which, with the images of Mary and John on either side, stood on top of the Rood screen beneath the chancel arch. After processing around the churchyard on Palm Sunday, the clergy and people entered the church and gathered before the screen. The veil was then drawn up on pulleys as the parish sank to its knees, an anthem was sung and the clergy venerated the revealed cross by kissing the ground. These and other practices, such as creeping to the cross, had been banned in 1547-8. By 1550 the churchwardens at

South side of Old St. Alkmund's

St. Mary's had disposed of their veil *'that hanged afore the Rood loft'*, although it seems to have been given away for safe keeping. Probably they hoped that the old ceremonies would soon be restored, and in that respect they were not disappointed. As the money spent on an Easter sepulchre in 1554 shows, Queen Mary's accession in the previous year brought about a brief revival of Catholic practices before they were again prohibited after 1558.

Before the Reformation, such practices were flourishing as never before, creating a rich devotional world. At the heart of this world was an intense belief in the value of good works, including bequests to the church, alms for the poor, and the pious provision of prayers and the sacrament of the mass. This commitment was rooted in the belief in Purgatory, a place of suffering to which souls pass after death to be made fit to enter heaven. The prospect of Purgatory was not necessarily a dreadful one. Not only was it preferable to the stark alternative between heaven and hell which had once been thought to exist, but it was also possible to shorten the time spent in Purgatory by penance and good works during life. One obvious sign of this emphasis on good works in late medieval Shrewsbury was the rebuilding of substantial parts of the parish churches in the 'perpendicular' style, such as the spire and clerestory at St. Mary's, the spire at St. Alkmund's and the upper part of the tower at St. Julian's. Surviving wills tell us that money was left for *'new building'* at both St. Mary's and St. Alkmunds's in the 1470s, while the mercer William Moyne also asked in 1499 to be buried in a new chapel in St. Alkmund's - probably in the perpendicular south aisle demolished with most of the old church in 1794. Work of similar date is also visible on an illustration of the south side of old St. Julian's before it was pulled down in 1748-9, leaving only the tower.

Another and particularly valuable way of building up a store of merit to shorten the pains of Purgatory was to endow a priest to sing mass not simply for oneself but for other Christian souls as well. These souls, it was thought, would also benefit from the priest's labours, provided they had showed themselves worthy during their own lives. A chantry or service of this kind could be financed either by an individual (like that founded in St. Mary's in 1469 by Richard Stury), or by a fraternity or guild. In the latter case, members believed that not only would their predecessors be assisted in Purgatory, but they in turn would also benefit after death. In this way the living and the dead were linked in a circle of mutual advantage. At least fourteen fraternities, each with its own wardens, existed in Shrewsbury during the early sixteenth century, although some of them were probably not wealthy enough to employ

South side of Old St. Julian's

St. Katherine and her wheel
(from a church carving)

a full-time priest, but simply maintained a candle or 'light' at one of the side altars. Six of them were set up by craft fellowships, but others such as the fraternities of the Holy Cross (in St. Alkmund's) and St. Katherine (in St. Julian's) may have been parish fraternities. The former had been founded in the fourteenth century by Thomas Pride, and it is thought that the chantry priest, a schoolmaster and the parish clerk may have resided in the complex of buildings at Bear Steps. There were two other fraternities dedicated to St. Katherine, one of the most popular saints in the late Middle Ages whose martyrdom was dramatized by a play in Shrewsbury in 1526.

Apart from everyday charity, the wealthy could also benefit their souls by endowing almshouses for the poor. St. Chad's almshouses on the south-east side of the churchyard had been founded in the early fifteenth century, but were administered by the Mercers from the 1460s.

St. Chad's almshouses

St. Mary's almshouses were founded later on the initiative of the draper Degory Watur in 1444. When he made his will in 1477 he left the rest of his estate to the Drapers to find a priest and look after the almspeople.

A drawing of 1823 suggests that the buildings originally consisted of a row of single-storey dwellings adjacent to a service hall, itself divided by a screens passage from the main hall in which the master lived. Watur himself had been master at one time, and by tradition he was said to have attended church with the inmates, sitting on *'a fair long pew made for them and himself'*. Twice a week the almspeople went to church to pray for their founders and benefactors, and once a week in the almshouses themselves.

Through the prayers of the poor, benefactors were helped to eventual salvation. The assistance of the saints in this respect was also highly valued. Images and pictures of the saints could be found throughout the churches, with lights burning before them. Court cases sometimes refer to the images as in 1516 when John ap Atha was sued for failing to paint an image of the Trinity in St. Alkmund's beside that of St. Giles, as he had promised to do. In 1530 the goldsmith Robert Heyffeld also brought an action because he had not been paid for gilding an image of Our Lady. The decoration on these images was extremely valuable and not surprisingly they were sometimes the target for thieves, as in 1520 when an image of Our Lady in St. Chad's was stripped of silver. Another insight into lay piety can be found in the rare, secular wall painting in the King's Head pub in Mardol, discovered in 1987. Dating from about 1450 to 1520, it includes a depiction of the Last Supper - an appropriate subject in what was once a hall used for eating.

The huge number of commemorative prayers and masses demanded by the laity meant that the role of the clergy was all-important. As collegiate churches, both St. Mary's and St. Chad's were in a good position to fulfil this demand. In addition to their own curates, these colleges together had about ten vicars choral who attended with their service books to these duties. But there were also 'stipendiary' priests who earned their living by tending particular services, such as Stury's chantry or the Drapers' Holy Trinity service. Judging from the evidence of pledge taking, some of these clerks or chaplains as they were

Seal of St. Mary's college

Seal of St. Chad's college

known were probably related to craftsmen in the town, like the chaplain Roger Ireland who was supported by the merchant David Ireland in a lawsuit in the Small Court in 1515.

Nine years later the shearman William Pickering also stood pledge for Giles Pickering, brother and later prior of the Austin Friars in Shrewsbury, suggesting another family connection. Although in the course of everyday business friars from all three religious houses were sometimes sued for debts and the Augustinians in particular were quite a rowdy lot, there is every indication that they were normally well regarded. Testators often left money to the friars in their wills, no doubt recollecting their help as confessors, and the bailiffs and burgesses gave them money to repair their houses. In addition, the town sometimes rewarded the friars for delivering public sermons, like that

Priest and friar taking confession

given in 1526 by Dr. Duffield, warden of the Franciscan Friars. He was a noted preacher who in the previous year had been licensed to preach in the diocese of Hereford, south of Shrewsbury. Anyone who came to hear him was granted an 'indulgence', reducing their future spell in Purgatory by forty days. Shrewsbury also possessed a hermitage at the Spelcross beyond Coleham on the Longden road, dedicated to St. Mary Magdalen. The hermit himself sometimes appeared in lawsuits in the Small Court, and a hermit was still in residence, presumably at this site, in 1538. Altogether, including the monks across the river at the abbey (numbering eighteen in 1540), there were over fifty priests, monks and friars administering to the religious needs of Salopians in the early sixteenth century.

'The virtue of the mass'

By faith alone

When the merchant David Ireland made his will in 1529, he asked to be buried in the Lady Chapel in St. Chad's. Every priest from the four parish churches was to attend, as well as representatives from the friaries. Twenty four candles weighing three pounds each, borne by twenty-four poor people wearing gowns, were to burn around his hearse, while the trental of St. Gregory, a popular series of thirty masses, often known as the Pope mass, was to be sung in his memory. Lights were left to the high altar and all the other side altars in St. Chad's, and £100 was given to buy lands to endow, if possible, a chantry *'for my soul, my wife's soul and all christian souls'.* Money was also given to the friars for a trental on the anniversary of his death, and to the vicars choral of St. Chad's to sing an annual commemoration or 'obit'. In addition £5 was left to the poor on his burial day. There is no better way of understanding what the protestant Reformation was about than by comparing this will with that made by the Shrewsbury draper John Mynton in 1549.

Basing his preamble upon a controversial will made by a Gloucestershire gentleman William Tracy in 1530 (much admired by the reformer William Tyndale), Mynton stated that;

> *'The ground of my belief is that there is but one mediator between god and man, which man, as Paul saith, is Christ Jesus, and therefore I will seek no other mean nor means to merit by, nor I do not bestow no part of my goods for that intent, for my merit is only the faith in Christ's blood'.*

As for his burial, Mynton continued in his own words;

> *'I will that no sacrifice of mass be done, for in that work the priest taketh on him the office of Christ, whereby the enemies of Christ's church have diminished Christ's passion and have trodden his blessed blood underfoot; and counted the*

word of his promise to be taken of none effect, and therefore that work of the mass is to be despised or rather to be abhorred of all those that professeth Christ. For as Saint Paul saith, Christ hath offered himself once for all; a sacrifice to God to take away the sins of many, and therefore they that take on them the office of Christ, and offer him up again art contrary to the doctrine of the Holy Ghost in Saint Paul, and also do despise that perfect work that Christ wrought out on the cross, sufficient for ever, and is now entered into heaven ever more to be sacrifice for sins'.

And so Mynton instructed that no dirge be sung at his funeral, but only the Te Deum and other godly psalms in English. Only the ministers of St. Chad's were to attend, each receiving 6d, and £1 was left to *'a godly, learned man'* to give three sermons in the church.

Our Lady of Pity, Battlefield church

For protestants like Mynton salvation was attained only by faith in Christ's single redeeming sacrifice and not by good works and the supposed eating of Christ's body in the mass. Purgatory itself was a vain invention and the laity could dispense with the army of confessors and priests administering the mass. The cult of the saints was simply superstition and images and pictures were no better than idols made of wood, stone, alabaster or paint.

The actual process of protestant reform took many years, and as we have seen

was briefly reversed during Queen Mary's reign. Images, lights, processions and practices such as creeping to the cross were banned in 1547-8, and the pictures of Our Lady in St. Mary's and Mary Magdalen in St. Chad's were burnt in the market place. No doubt among the other images destroyed was that of Our Lady of Pity in St. Chad's, mentioned in the will of Alderman Richard Brickdale in 1543, which, like the wooden image which survives in Battlefield church, would have shown Mary holding the body of Christ across her lap after his removal from the cross. The three friaries had already been dissolved in 1538, followed by the abbey in 1540. The chantries and fraternities were also suppressed in 1547-8 and their lands, with those of the collegiate churches, were seized by the Crown, as were later all the parish goods, like vestments and chalices, that had been used in the old Catholic rites.

The five wounds of Christ

Yet the evidence in Shrewsbury, as elsewhere, suggests that Salopians were not at first greatly attracted to reform. Men like Mynton were exceptional. More typical were those like the weaver Roger Kingley, who in the same year as Mynton made his will, had left a votive offering of 5d to the five wounds of Christ and 5d for the five joys of Our Lady - one of the most popular devotions of the old religion. When Queen Mary came to the throne in 1553, the churchwardens were happy enough to restore the rites and fittings of catholic religion. At St. Mary's, for example, the rood loft was repaired, the Easter sepulchre rebuilt, a new pyx and other fittings were purchased, and the great high altar of stone (hated by the reformers as an object of superstition) was restored. But it was to no avail. In 1561-2 the rood cross and the upper part of the loft were taken down again, followed in 1565 by the beam on which the cross was mounted. By 1573 a carpenter was once again employed to make a frame for a communion table in place of the altar stone. Some objects lasted longer. The churchyard crosses which had been part of the processional route on Palm Sunday were not taken down until 1581-5. Behind the carvings on St. Chad's cross a candle was found, *'offered by some superstitious person'* as the chronicler put it.

Like most English people, Salopians conformed to the Reformation out of inertia or respect for the Crown and its authority. Successful resistance was in any case impossible. At the same time wealthier residents saw an unprecedented opportunity to take part in the greatest land grab since the Norman Conquest, as the Crown sold off the lands it had confiscated to finance its crazy wars. Among those who benefited were the Irelands (the abbey estate at Albrighton), the Langleys (the abbey site), the Edwardeses (St. Chad's College site) and the Popes (the friaries). In the latter case the barrister Roger Pope had by the 1600s begun to block off the rights of way to or through the friaries, provoking much litigation with the corporation. He was also alleged to have stripped the battlements off the ancient round tower near the Austin Friars and to have turned it into a tanning room, while a defensive blockhouse behind the friary was said to have been converted into a dovecot.

The manor of the Abbey Foregate itself, which included the home farm of the abbey, was not sold until 1578. The three big families in the Abbey Foregate - Prynce, Rocke and Hatton - had all cast eyes upon it. Much of the land was already leased by them from the manor. Richard Prynce had a lease of the

The round tower

The Trill mill

Trill mill on the Rea brook (at the end of Mill Road in Abbey Foregate). With his legal connections in London, he was in a good position to hear the latest rumours about impending sales, and at the right moment quietly sneaked down to the capital to arrange a purchase. But his neighbours Thomas Hatton and Thomas Rocke got word of his movements from their friends. They were alarmed that if Prynce bought the manor he might start to question the legality of their leases, being a man *'much given to search into other men's titles'*, as they later put it. They hastily rode up to London to confront Prynce in person. He sheepishly suggested that they purchase the manor together, and after the Crown had first sold it to a pair of speculators, they re-purchased it *'for a great sum of money'*. This was the other side of the Reformation - covetousness and naked greed.

The godly minister

A city on the hill?

The protestant Reformation in England was officially established by the religious settlement after 1559. Now that the laity could no longer rely upon a religion of images and the drama of the mass, a learned ministry to preach God's word from the Bible was needed more than ever. As in towns all over England, the burgesses began to support a public preacher, although in Shrewsbury he always served as minister of St. Mary's as well. Much effort was spent devising ways to provide him and other preachers in town with a decent income. By 1600 the public preacher was paid a respectable £46 13s 4d a year (on top of his salary of about £20 as minister), and had prestigious lodgings in the Drapers' Hall. To employ a noted preacher was a matter of local pride. When John Tomkys died in 1592, for example, the bailiffs described him as the *'golden candlestick of doctrine which hath shined amongst us now divers years'*. To increase the impact of preaching, a common practice grew up in towns known as the exercise. District clergy would gather together in one of the town churches, often on market day, and take a turn to deliver a lecture. Exercises had begun in St. Chad's by 1574, and in March 1575 masters in the Mercers' company were told by the bailiffs to attend them all. The Council in the Marches are also known to have been present on occasion.

Every protestant could agree upon the need for a godly ministry. But some wanted to go further. They felt that Christians should conform totally to the word of God in the Bible, applying its sense to the whole of religious and daily life, even where the scriptures offered no specific guidance. When Queen Elizabeth insisted, for example, that some vestments should still be worn by ministers during services, they objected bitterly. It was true that scripture had nothing to say about this matter but wearing vestments did not conform to the spirit of true religion. There was obviously some sympathy for this view in Shrewsbury. Some ministers refused to wear their cross caps and surplices until 1573 and the practice remained unpopular. When diocesan officials visited the town in 1589 to check that services were in order they again had to instruct that surplices should be worn; but the ministers simply waited until they had gone before once more discarding the 'rags of Rome'.

Those who disliked neuter Christians, and felt deeply that godliness should inform one's whole life, came to be known as puritans. It was an imprecise term, often used as a term of abuse rather like the words 'fascist' or 'racist' are today. When, for example, the currier Thomas Henckesman got involved in a quarrel with Widow Whitcott in 1629, he called her a *'lying puritan lady'*, adding *'a pox of all puritans and a pox of god on such puritans as thou art'*. The labourer John Evans also tangled with his neighbour Thomas Hodges in Coleham in January 1620, challenging him to a fight in the street. But Hodges refused and went indoors. Evans then bawled through the flimsy wall that separated them, *'Thou come out of a puritan's house and I come out of a papist's house and if thou will, I will play at cards with thee for a pot of ale'*. Hodges shouted back that he didn't know any puritans. *'I know a papist's house'*, Evans answered, *'and I love the papists and I pray God bless them and I will stand with them while I live'*. It was all drunken bravado, but it shows how 'puritan' came to be used as a word of derision. With their air of pious superiority, the unspotted lambs of the Lord were an obvious target for alehouse sarcasm.

Puritans wanted to build a community of sober godly Christians which would stand like a shining city on the hill, and even less zealous magistates might lend some support. Church attendance once a week had been a traditional obligation, reinforced by statute in 1559, but more than this was needed. In 1581 it was agreed on the advice of the public preacher Edward Bulkeley that morning service would be held at 8 a.m. in St. Chad's, 9 a.m. in St. Julian's and 10 a.m. in St. Mary's, giving everyone a chance to attend at least one. In 1586 the Mercers' company were also instructed that one person from every household must attend divine service on Tuesdays and Thursdays. The enforcement of the Sabbath in particular became an obsession, with Salopians

regularly presented for failing to attend church, usually because they were stuck in the alehouses, playing games like shovel-board and nine-holes. A typical incident occurred in May 1619 when a group of morris dancers

Morris dancing

were arrested for absenting themselves from evening prayer on Sunday and trying to stick their lord of misrule in the stocks for a lark. In practice a really good attendance at church only ever occurred at Easter communion, as the huge quantities of communion wine that had to be purchased then demonstrates. In 1622 over three gallons of wine were bought by the churchwardens of St. Julian's for the two services on Easter day.

Supervision of sexual behaviour also became tighter, and there was a marked increase by 1600 in the number of people bound over for moral offences. John Gardener, who was brought before the sessions in 1582 for getting his maidservant pregnant, suffered a typical fate. He was ordered to appear at Sunday evensong in St. Mary's dressed in the traditional white sheet

Whipping behind the cart

Of those who tried to build the godly city in Shrewsbury, John Tomkys was perhaps the most impressive. A native of Bilston in Staffordshire, Tomkys served as public preacher from 1582 until his death in 1592. He was a learned man who had translated books by the Swiss reformer Bullinger, and published a catechism on the Lord's prayer in 1585. We can guess that like other godly ministers of his time, Tomkys would also have cultivated a great beard evoking the prophets of the Old Testament. He was fortunate in that

The godly household, 1560

of penance - a public humiliation also imposed on occasion by the church courts and the Council in the Marches. Another kind of punishment was that inflicted upon the maidservant Elinor Bland in 1593 for bearing a bastard son of her master William Hill of Shelton, and for adultery with two other married men. Like a vagabond, she was carted through the town and then despatched to her place of birth - the standard punishment for 'whoring'. If she ever dared to return, she would be put into the cage and whipped in public on the next market day.

The town was full of snoopers and malicious accusations of adultery. In 1635 Lucy Ranson told the bailiffs that she had peered through a key hole into an adjoining chamber and saw Ursula Jones lying naked on the bed with a butcher. The spinster Sara Jones chipped in that Ursula sometimes came back from the alehouse in such a stupor that she was unable to undress herself, slumping instead all night on the bed in her clothes. In the next year Widow Everall, who kept an alehouse in Coleham, scornfully told a housewife that she *went out empty bellied from her husband and came home full bellied*, and held up two fingers like horns - the sign of the cuckold and the origin of the V sign still used today.

St. Mary's parish was a 'peculiar' jurisdiction, one, that is, which was not subject to the bishop's supervision. This meant that it had its own church court which Tomkys presided over, and which he could use to enforce a moral and religious reformation. Already the interior walls of St. Mary had been whitewashed and painted with the Ten Commandments; but now the organs were sold off to the Dean of Worcester, and the churchwardens were ordered to remove from the north window a last superstitious depiction of the Assumption of the Blessed Virgin Mary.

Tomkys also prepared a set of articles enquiring into every aspect of parochial life - just as the diocesan bishop had done in 1584. As well as their own duty to attend church, keep the Sabbath and send their children every Sunday morning for catechism, parishioners were instructed to keep an eye open for any sign of catholicism such as the use of beads, crossings and *'such other vain popish trash'*. Hostility was also shown to a host of popular customs which threatened godly rule, including morris dancing, Christmas mumming, lords of misrule, saints' day ringings, and the use of wizards and cunning women. Ancient beliefs about childbirth and burial were also suspect. Midwives, for instance, were to be watched to see if they resorted to charms and superstitions, such as asking for all chests and doors to be unlocked during the delivery. Many of these articles expressed a strong yet conventional protestant piety: but there is no doubt that Tomkys wished to press godly reform further, as his opposition to the Shearmen's tree shows.

But moral reformation proved difficult to secure. For one thing, as we saw in chapter 7, the life of the alehouse proved impossible to suppress. For another, it is clear that some members of the town élite supported the sociable nature of the old customs. The behaviour of the bailiffs during the dispute over the Shearmen's tree, for example, was bitterly attacked by the auditors who felt that the treatment of Fernes and his colleagues had been completely out of order; and it was the town recorder who allowed the custom to continue. Similarly, in the early seventeenth century actors were still being permitted by some bailiffs to perform in town (unlike in other places), and it was the town clerk Thomas Owen who staunchly defended the customary disorders on Election night as a *'privilege of the people'*. Many of these customs helped townsfolk to relate their lives to every other. Banning them left a void which still needed to be filled in some way. The fate of the old Corpus Christi procession shows this well.

From Corpus Christi to Shrewsbury Show

In Shrewsbury the Corpus Christi procession continued to be held until 1547 when processions to celebrate the mass were banned by the Crown. The Mercers' records show that there may have been a brief revival for a few years after 1554, but then it disappeared, along with other customs such as the maytime Abbot and walk-abouts by the bailiffs on All Saints'

The Shoemaker's arbour in 1864

day. Even the stage for the Whitsun plays seems to have been dismantled in 1575. Between 1564 and 1606 at least five of the craft fellowships altered their rules to eradicate the *'superstitious'* articles that had specified arrangements for Corpus Christi day. But the memory may have lingered on as an incident in 1591 reveals. On the Sunday after Richard Fernes and the other shearmen had been arrested for bringing in their tree, John Tomkys was returning home from visiting a sick resident of St. Chad's parish. Forty apprentice shearmen, led by a blind musician, began to dog his steps. Every time Tomkys stopped at a corner to ask what was going on, they stopped too. Every time he walked on, they followed; and *'in this mocking and flouting manner'* as the bailiffs complained, escorted him to his house at Drapers' Hall. They then marched around St. Mary's churchyard, with the minstrel playing before them, *'according to the old order of procession'* - a gross provocation since Tomkys's articles had specifically challenged irreverent piping and dancing in the churchyard on the Sabbath.

Corpus Christi had not only been a great religious festival but also a lynch-pin in the life of the companies. Although the procession had gone, the need to define life in that way still remained. At some time about 1600, the companies began to parade to their arbours on Kingsland for a day of eating and good fellowship, but this time not on Corpus Christi day but on the following Monday. The origins of this festival, which came to be known as Shrewsbury Show, are obscure although it was once said to have begun in 1591. Between 1597 and 1599 the Weavers purchased a banner which may have been meant for use on that occasion, like the flag and arms of Minerva which they had acquired by 1625, and which were certainly used in the parade in later years. Significantly too, the company moved its election day to Show day in 1609, as did the Glovers' company in 1614. On that day also it was put to the Shearmen's company in 1620 that they should go *'brotherly'* to Kingsland for a dinner. By the 1680s some of the company arbours had become substantial structures - like that of the Shoemakers with its timber hall and elaborate stone archway (now in the Dingle) erected in 1679, with the statues of their patron saints Crispin and Crispinian on either side. The Show had become one of the principal occasions in the Salopian calendar.

But there was one great difference between the Show and the old Corpus Christi procession. Neither the Drapers' nor the Mercers' companies ever took part. In the old catholic religion, townsfolk had been encouraged to live in peace, charity and unity with one another - that was one of the meanings of the mass and of Corpus Christi itself. By 1600, it seems, some of the richer craftsmen no longer appreciated this, and had begun to withdraw from the customs of the people.

Epilogue

Memory and place

Nearly four weeks after Richard Fernes and his colleagues had finally been released for fetching in the Shearmen's tree, John Banks came to the Shrewsbury assizes with his famous dancing horse Morocco, thought to be alluded to by Moth in Shakespeare's *Love's Labour Lost* (Act 1, Scene 2). By tapping its hoof it could tell how many pieces of money there were in a man's purse, or indicate the numbers on the upper face of a pair of dice, and perform many other similar tricks. When Banks told his horse, '*Sir, ha, there be two bailiffs in this town, the one of them did bid me welcome into the town and used me in friendly manner, I would have thee go to him and give thanks for me*', the horse trotted up to Bailiff Sherer and bowed before him. Many watchers thought that Banks must have been using a 'familiar' - an imp or spirit which wizards and witches could turn into animal form. The idea was not so different from the popular belief that maladies were caused by evil spirits which could be transferred by magic from one carrier to another. In 1580, for example, the 'cunning woman' Mother Gawen of Castle Foregate tried unsuccessfully to draw the spirit from a neighbour's sick sow into her cat. Such magic was frowned upon by both protestant and catholic authorities. Gawen herself was punished in the Cornmarket pillory, while Banks later narrowly escaped being accused of witchcraft after displaying his horse in France.

For the watching crowd, Banks's visit became a memory fixed to a certain place. The experience of that place is linked to the succession of these memories. Many events could have turned

Banks's dancing horse

into memories of that kind - the royal camel brought to town in 1526; the fierce blaze in 1557 at Bennett's Hall, caused by a baker's faggots catching fire, which burnt itself out within the ancient walls; the gosling hatched in 1569 at the house of Edward Mynton in Frankwell with four feet and a head like a swan; the cleft-footed York boy without nipples displayed at the June fair in 1580; the giant Fleming from Antwerp, 7 1/2 feet tall, who stayed at Thomas Mytton's house (the Red Lion inn of which Mytton was the tenant) in April 1582, and who was later robbed of all his money; or the remains of a child with two heads and two backbones exhibited in a coffin by a London showman in July 1583. Memorable too was the visit in July 1590 of a troupe of acrobats called The Queen's Men, including a Hungarian tight-rope walker who performed with his balancing pole (weighing 38 pounds) upon a rope strung across the Cornmarket.

Many fatal accidents also stuck in the mind such as the death of the son of John Davies the brewer in 1539. A sudden gust of wind had blown the gates together just as he was passing through the Welsh Gate, crushing his skull and splashing his brains across the bridge. In July 1597 Alderman Thomas Stury also met a tragic end after being rowed upstream to the family home at Rossall; as he put a foot ashore, the boat suddenly slipped away beneath him and he fell backwards into the Severn and was drowned. Suicides too provoked much local gossip. When the young wife of a Chilton (Atcham) tailor hanged herself in November 1574, using her husband's bow-string, people recalled that her parents had been bitterly opposed to her marriage. Shortly after the wedding she had met her father by chance and had knelt down before him for his blessing; but he had turned his back on her and had walked away, *'the which unkindness people judge was the occasion of her death'.* Other incidents were happier to recall. On St. David's day in 1633 the barber Richard Leather hung out a guy from his house at the High Cross, attaching to it a giant leek, *'in despite of the Welshmen'.* That would have had them chortling in the alehouses. So too the antics of George Arthur, a lame steeplejack from St. Albans, hired to re-point the steeple of St. Alkmund's in February and March 1585. When the weather cock was restored, he stood upon the iron cross, twirling the cock about and shaking his legs and arms out in the wind and rain. On another day he stood upright upon the cross, shot an arrow from a long bow and tapped away on a drum. As his manner was, he would go up drunk in hob-nailed boots but come down sober.

These were human events, but natural ones also stuck in the mind. In November 1575 residents were astonished to discover a red deer wandering near Roushill lane; it was caught and brought to the bailiffs. Then there were the comets of 1577 and 1580, and the remarkable displays of the northern lights, Aurora Borealis, observed on eight occasions alone between 1564 and 1574. The Severn too brought its immemorial floods. During the great flood of Michaelmas 1586 Salopians were transfixed by the sight of a dung heap floating by with several pigs on it walking up and down. Downstream it broke apart and all the swine were drowned. On Saturday 10 January 1596 the water reached two feet deep in the Myntons' house in Frankwell, and the family was forced upstairs until Monday morning, a fate familiar to generations of residents in that suburb which was inundated on nine occasions between 1576 (when a barge was punted through the street) and 1602. Christmas 1601 was a particularly watery one: *'it troubled them sore in washing down their walls, ovens and furnaces to their great hindrance and losses beside'.* Other natural phenomena also still recur. Anyone in Shrewsbury on 2 April 1990 will remember the earthquake that shook the town at ten minutes to three in the afternoon, caused by a deep fault that runs beneath south Shropshire. Perhaps it was the same fault that produced the quake at 4 p.m. on 26 February 1575 followed by two hours of after-shocks. Books fell off shelves, pigeons and crows took to the air, and *'a dead, thundering noise'* was heard within the ground. In some ways still, nature continues to link Shrewsbury to its past.

Subject Index

Abbey, ... 11, 41, 63-4, 67, 103-05
Abbot, ... 9-10, 64
Affrays and bloods,... 53-5
Aldermen, ... 7, 15-18, 22, 27
Alehouses/alesellers, ... 4, 46-7, 50, 52, 79, 81, 89, 107-09, 112
Almshouses, ... 11, 48, 54, 101
Appeal of felony, ... 91-4
Apprenticeship, ... 41-4
Arbours, ... 50, 110
Archery, ... 50, 81, 87
Assize (of bread and ale), ... 77, 79-81
Assizes (judicial), ... 2, 49, 92, 95
Attorneys, ... 14, 57, 60-1, 65-7, 98
Auditors, ... 15, 19, 109

Bailiffs, ... 1-3, 6-18, 20, 22, 51-2, 54-9, 64, 68, 70, 73-4,
... ... 77-9, 81, 84, 90-4, 97, 106, 109, 111-12
Bakers, ... 77-9
Bargemen, ... 75, 77, 84-6
Bars, ... 9
Bells, ... 5-6
Benefit: of belly, ... 94
      of Clergy, ... 94-5
Brewers,... ... ... 13, 77, 79-81, 85
Bribsters, ... 79-81
Bricks/brickmakers, ... 83-4
Bridges: Coleham, ... 64, 78
      Monks', ... 64
      Stone, ... 19, 23, 53-4, 64, 84-6, 95, 98
      Welsh, ... 27, 43, 46, 53, 63, 85-6, 91, 98
Bridle, ... 53
Bull-baiting, ... 9, 78, 86
Bundling, ... 45
Burgages, ... 19, 31, 71
Burgesses, ... 18-21, 46, 48, 78, 80, 85
Bushels, ... 32
Butchers, ... 34, 77-9

Cages, ... 98, 108
Calendar, ... 6-12
Candles, ... 34, 78, 83
Capping, ... 76-7
Carpentry, ... 82-4
Carriers, ... 32, 74
Carting, ... 108

Castle, ... 2, 8, 40, 86
Chamber of Concord, ... 17
Chamberlain, ... 15
Chantries, ... 100-01, 103-04
Churches/parishes:
      St Alkmunds, ... 5, 26-7, 34, 47, 100-01, 112
      St Chad, ... 5, 9, 11, 17, 26, 45, 90-01, 101, 103-07, 109
      St Julian, ... 5-6, 9, 47, 100-01, 107
      St Mary, ... 5, 7, 9-10, 27, 29, 54, 77, 83, 99-101, 104-110
Clocks, ... 3
Cloth trade, ... 25, 42, 45, 69, 73-5
Cloth markets (Oswestry, Welshpool), ... 5, 20, 25, 34, 45, 74, 90
Coal, ... 38, 85
Cock-fighting, ... 9, 87
Commons (burgesses), ... 18-22
Commons (pasture), ... 6, 19, 23, 97
Companies, ... 48-50, 92, 97, 110
Conduit, ... 5, 19-20, 37, 58
Constables, ... 20, 31, 51-2, 60, 90
Cooks, ... 51, 81
Coroners, ... 15, 53, 91, 93
Corpus Christi, ... 7, 10-11, 45, 49-50, 76, 81, 109-110
Council Chamber, ... 16-17, 19
Council in the Marches, ... 9-10, 17, 40, 49, 67, 71, 73, 76
... ... 95-8, 106, 108
Councillors, ... 7, 15-18, 21-2
Counsellors (barristers), ... 66-8, 96
Courting, ... 45-6
Courts: Great, ... 14, 23, 51-2, 59, 64, 79, 83, 89
      Small, ... 14, 27, 57, 59-60, 64-5, 67, 73, 84-5
Craft masters, ... 43-4
Credit, ... 23, 25, 60
Crier, ... 3, 17
Curfew, ... 3, 14, 98

Daggers,... 56
Dearth, ... 37, 78-9, 81
Demurrers, ... 66
Diet, ... 79
Distraint, ... 61
Dowry, ... 45-6
Drapers' Hall, ... 28, 37, 106, 109
Drunkenness, ... 14
Dyers, ... 37, 69, 85

Earthquakes,	112
Easter sepulchre,	99, 105
Election night,	12, 21, 41, 97, 109
Enclosures,	4, 58
Engrossing,	77, 85
Estreats,	52
Essoins,	61
Exchequer,	16, 37, 52, 58-9, 61, 86, 90-1
Exercises,	106
Fairs,	19, 23, 27, 36, 89, 112
Felonies,	89
Fencing,	21, 86
Fires,	83
Fishmongers/fishing,	34, 86
Flesh (meat) boards,	26, 34, 78
Floats,	85-6
Floods,	64-5, 112,
Football,	8, 86
Forestalling,	35, 52
Fraternities,	48, 100-01, 104
Friaries/friars,	5, 9, 19, 50, 53, 66, 85, 91, 102-05
Fulling,	76
Gallows,	94-5
Gambling,	87-8, 90
Gaoler,	13, 65
Gates,	3-4, 26, 35-6
Burgess/Castle,	2, 19, 38, 56, 62, 64-5
Postern,	2, 4, 53, 98
Stone,	62, 64-5
Welsh,	14, 31, 40, 46, 62-4, 112
Guildhall (Booth Hall),	16-17, 19, 21, 51, 59, 68, 90, 92, 94
Guilds,	48-9
Gumblestool,	53
Guns,	87
Harvest,	12, 77-8
Hawking,	87
Hermitage,	9, 88, 103
Holidays,	6, 41
Christmas,	7-8, 12
Easter,	8, 44, 87
Whitsun,	8-10
Hops,	80
Horse racing,	87
Hospitals,	48, 67
Households,	37, 47, 49
Housing,	71-2
Hue and cry,	91
Images,	101, 104, 106
Income,	20
Indictments,	2, 93-4
Inns,	34
Raven,	15
Red Lion,	54, 91, 95, 112

Unicorn,	74
Inquests,	31
Coroner's,	15, 93, 95
For damages,	68
Great,	51-2, 54-5, 58, 93
Little,	52
Juries,	2, 67-8
Common/special,	68
Grand,	22, 93, 97
Petty,	93-4, 97
Journeymen,	37, 44-5, 47
Kingsland,	4, 19, 27, 50, 81, 95, 110
Labourers,	37, 70, 79
Latrines,	53
Leasors,	68
Liberties,	17, 32, 52, 64
Lighting,	3-4, 6
Lords of misrule,	7-9, 107, 109
Maidservants,	43
Maps,	23, 64, 69, 77, 84-5
Mardol quay,	85
Market gardening,	79
Market Hall,	32, 34, 62-3, 92
Markets/marketing,	23, 25, 27, 32-7, 52, 78
Marriage,	45, 47
Mass,	7, 103-04, 106, 110
Maypoles,	9, 20
Maze,	50
Members of parliament,	19, 67, 70, 73
Mercers' Hall,	21
Mills: corn,	19-20, 57, 86, 95, 106
fulling,	76
Misdemeanours,	89, 94
Mudholes,	53
Mummers,	7, 9, 109
Neck verse,	94
Nightwalkers,	4
Occupations,	69-70
Pasture behind the walls,	4, 12, 19
Peace bonds,	56-7
Pesthouse,	27
Petitions,	13-15
Pigs,	79
Pillory,	91-2, 96, 111
Plague,	25-7
Plays,	9-10, 40, 49, 86, 89-90, 101, 109
Pleading,	59, 66-7
Pledges (sureties),	56-7, 60-2, 64, 76, 101-02
Poor,	31, 34, 38, 77, 79, 81, 93, 103
Population growth,	23

Presentments,	...	...	...	...	...	52-4, 77, 80, 93
Price of corn,	...	...	...	...	...	78-9
Prisons,	...	...	...	...	...	62-6, 91, 94
Privies,	...	...	...	...	...	53
Prostitution,	...	...	...	...	...	53-4
Public preachers,	...	...	...	...	...	1, 95, 106-08
Purgatory,	...	...	...	...	...	100, 103-04
Puritans,	...	...	...	...	...	6, 20, 81, 107
Quarry,	...	...	...	...	...	9, 19, 89
Recorder,	...	...	...	...	...	2, 59, 109
Recreations,	...	...	...	...	...	86-8
Reformation,	...	...	5-7, 12, 45, 48-9, 64, 99-100, 103, 106, 109
Regrating,	...	...	...	...	...	52
Rents,	...	...	...	...	...	67, 71, 78, 90
Rights of way,	...	...	...	...	...	19
River workers,	...	...	...	...	...	86
Sabbatarianism,	...	...	...	...	...	6, 34, 77, 107, 109
St Winifred,	...	...	...	...	...	11, 63
Sanctuary,	...	...	...	...	...	91
Saving harmless,	...	...	...	...	...	61-2
Scarlet days,	...	...	...	...	...	7
School,	...	...	19-20, 28, 38-41, 62, 69, 73, 81, 92
Scolds,	...	...	...	...	...	53
Seasons,	...	...	...	...	...	6
Sergeants,	...	...	2, 14-15, 21, 52, 61-2, 64, 68, 81, 90-1
Servants,	...	...	...	...	...	37
Sessions of the peace,	...	...	...	...	2, 57, 91-2, 94, 107
Sessors,	...	...	...	...	...	15, 46
Shaving,	...	...	...	...	...	6, 34
Shearing,	...	...	...	...	...	42, 74-6
Shearmen's tree,	...	...	1-2, 9, 13-14, 22, 92, 109, 111
Shoemakers,	...	...	...	...	...	49, 71
Shops,	...	...	...	...	43-5, 49, 71, 76, 81, 86
Shrewsbury Show,	...	...	...	...	...	110
Shuts,	...	...	...	...	...	30-1
Spout,	...	...	...	...	...	53
Steward,	...	...	...	...	...	94, 97
Stillyard,	...	...	...	...	...	21
Stocks,	...	...	...	...	...	91, 94

Streeters/streeters' bills,	...	...	...	12, 51-4, 77, 79-80, 86, 93
Suicide,	...	...	...	...	...	112
Suit lists,	...	...	...	...	...	51
Swannery,	...	...	...	...	...	98
Swine-keepers,	...	...	...	...	...	52
Taking the wall,	...	...	...	...	...	55
Tales men,	...	...	...	...	...	68
Tanning,	...	...	...	...	...	70, 85
Taverns,	...	...	...	...	...	4
Gullet,	...	...	...	...	...	11, 56, 86
Sextry,	...	...	...	...	...	11, 21, 37, 49
Teasels,	...	...	...	...	...	75, 85
Tensors,	...	...	...	...	...	20
Tenters,	...	...	...	...	...	75
Thornes' meadow,	...	...	...	...	...	19
Tickets,	...	...	...	...	...	61
Tilers,	...	...	...	...	...	83
Tokens,	...	...	...	...	...	36
Tolls,	...	...	...	7-8, 23, 25, 27, 36, 78-9, 85
Towers: Garewald's,	...	...	...	...	...	19
Round,	...	...	...	...	...	105
Town clerk,	...	...	22, 52, 58, 59, 61, 64, 66, 67, 91, 93, 109
Trials: civil,	...	...	...	...	...	68
criminal,	...	...	...	...	...	94
Turns: for the commons,	...	...	...	...	19
for the watch,	...	...	...	...	...	4
Victualling,	...	...	...	...	...	77-9
Wager of law,	...	...	...	...	...	67-8
Waits,	...	...	...	...	...	6, 8
Walls,	...	...	...	...	...	31
Wards,	...	...	...	...	4, 15, 62, 68, 83, 98
Wasters (cudgels),	...	...	...	...	...	21, 41, 86
Watch,	...	...	...	...	3-6, 26, 46, 90, 98
Weavers' Hall,	...	...	...	...	...	45
Weaving,	...	...	...	...	...	69, 75-6
Weirs,	...	...	...	...	...	86
Wool trade,	...	...	...	...	...	72-4, 78
Work hours,	...	...	...	...	...	5-6, 41

Suggestions For Further Reading

J. Barry (ed.), *The Tudor and Stuart Town* (1990)

P. Clark (ed.), *The Early Modern Town* (1976)

H. Swanson, *Medieval Artisans* (1989)

E. Duffy, *The Stripping of the Altars* (1992)

P. Collinson, *The Birthpangs of Protestant England* (1988)

R. W. Brunskill, *Housing* (1982)

C. Dyer, *Standards of living in the later Middle Ages* (1989)

Rev. W. A. Leighton (ed.), 'Early Chronicles of Shrewsbury' in *Transactions of the Shropshire Archaeological Society,* Vol. III (1880)

A. Somerset, *Records of Early English Drama. Shropshire* (forthcoming)

More books on Shrewsbury published by Shropshire Books

Shuts & Passages of Shrewsbury
A. Scott-Davies and R. S. Sears   £2.95

Everyday Life in Medieval Shrewbury
Dorothy Cromarty   £6.99

Shrewsbury Then and Now   £5.25